Growing Hemp For Profit

By **Paul Benhaim**

With **Shaun Bailey** & **Klara Marosszeky**

www.GrowingHempForProfit.com

About The Author

Paul Benhaim is a recognized world-authority in hemp research and development, as well as a published author of Hemp-related books and DVDs. He manages the world's most popular Hemp web sites and advises a number of international companies.

As well as acting as an independent consultant and mentor to those interested in business, usually the hemp business, Paul is CEO and Director of a cutting edge Hemp companies involved with hemp plastic and hemp food products.

Paul continues his quest to ensure the path for the widespread use of industrial hemp is accessible to all so new and revolutionary Hemp products may become available to a worldwide audience.

Born in London, after travelling the world for a decade, Paul now lives and works from his rainforest home in coastal Australia.

For further information on some of Paul's projects enjoy: www.hemp.co.uk and www.hempplastic.com

DISCLAIMER

This book is intended to help you decide if you want to start a hemp business. This book is not intended to be the only business you receive. You are recommended in this book to write a business plan. You should check all the data and facts are up to date and relevant to your location, state and federal laws. It is also strongly recommended that you speak with your lawyer, accountant and bank manager before moving ahead with any business. You may want to consider a personal business mentor as well.

Table of Contents

Introduction

You probably know all about hemp, whether it is from one of my books - Modern Introduction To Hemp, Healthy Eating Made Possible (H.E.M.P.) or somewhere else. If you don't then I recommend reading more about what hemp is and it's potential first, then come back and start here.

So, you want to grow some hemp – where do you start?

Knowing what you want, and why is always a good start. Hemp offers a potentially lucrative alternative to regular crops. It also offers a crop that may be up-valued on farm and sold independently of larger contractors. I recommend you start by knowing clearly why you want to grow, and then what you want to grow for. Know your market.

As Lewis Carroll once wrote: *One day Alice came to a fork in the road and saw a Cheshire cat in a tree. "Which road do I take?" she asked. "Where do you want to go?" was his response. "I don't know," Alice answered. "Then," said the cat, "it doesn't matter."*

The purpose of this book is to empower you in your choice.

You will find up-to-date information in this book on cultivating hemp, from in both the Northern and Southern Hemispheres. Most of the information here has been gathered by people who have been growing hemp for over 10 years. There is information for the smallholder or hobby farmer – specific cultivation tips, though much of this will be relevant to those interested in cultivating larger amounts of industrial hemp farmer.

You will find interviews with myself and two competent and globally experienced hemp farmers. This book would not be what it is without the help of both Shaun and Klara. I trust you will enjoy the results of this as much as I did in creating it.

As this book was intended to be written as an e-book you may want to check in with me from time to time to see if there are any updates at www.growinghempforprofit.com

Hempfully yours,

Paul

Let us begin

I have decided to start with an interview with my good friend, and long-time colleague Shaun Bailey. Shaun is based in Victoria in Australia, though a lot of what we talk about is quite generic. Later on you will find facts and figures, specific grow guides, including information specifically for the UK, Canada and other parts of the world. There is also a specific 'cultivation manual' for Australia. However, I always love the personal touch and in this interview I hope you will enjoy the dry Aussie humour that Shaun is so great with in person. Shaun is an expert and I predict will be one of the great leaders of the growing hemp industry.

Interview with Shaun Bailey

Shaun has been actively involved in the hemp industry since 2002 and researching since 1998. In this time Shaun has developed a business that looks likely to change the face of Australian hemp, and possibly the world hemp industry for ever... Read this interview for tips, secrets and overall wisdom of one of the hemp industries main players in the Southern Hemisphere. This interview was written in June, 2010.

P= Paul Benhaim
S= Shaun Bailey

P: Could we start by telling me your qualifications and what got you interested in hemp originally

S: I obtained an Associate Diploma in Applied Science majoring in Agronomy and a Certificate in Agriculture from the University of Queensland Gatton College. I graduated in 1994, worked with a large multinational cotton company in both the processing or ginning side, and also as an agronomist, focusing solely on cotton, where I worked my way through the company to a senior position in the business looking after the Upper Namoi region of NSW. Obviously I had an interest in fibres or I wouldn't have got involved with cotton. I grew up on large wheat and sheep property in western QLD and my first job after leaving school was working in shearing sheds which soon led to an interest in wool, another great natural fibre. We also had our own sheep and I used to work very closely with our professional wool classier and learnt to recognize the finer wool from the coarser wool. So I guess my interest in natural fibres goes right back to my early years. Whilst I was working with cotton, I obtained good access to world fibre market information and what fibre markets were growing and what wasn't growing and one area that I identified as a growth target was the bast fibre industry and that led me into more research into that particular industry and I isolated certain bast fibre crops to focus on. I did a lot more research and understood crops such as industrial hemp which yielded much higher bast fibre content on a per hectare basis than any other bast fibre crop and that's obviously led me to further research into companies to work with in this country.

P: So, that has led you to a company you have today called Planet Fibre Industries. Is there anything you can tell me about the background of Planet Fibre, how it started and what you are doing with it in Australia?

S: Planet Fibre was incorporated on 13th Feb. 2006, as a result of extensive amounts of research and development I undertook in Europe and the financial losses that I was incurring as a result, and I had to look at a way to make this business work and become profitable to recoup some of my earlier losses. I guess Planet Fibre really started to come together after my various trips to Europe and the seasons spent where I worked with BAFA from Malsch in Germany. Bernd Frank and Peter Muthmann took me under their wings and showed me what the requirements were to create a natural bast fibre industry in Australia. They shared their mistakes and showed me what they thought the opportunities were worth exploring; I came back and shared some of my findings with the Queensland department of Primary Industries and more recently with the Victorian department of Primary Industries and Regional Development Victoria to allow those government bodies involved; to understand the various protocols and procedures that were required for this industry to establish.

P: What are the top three things that someone should know in order to successfully grow their own hemp?

S: Certainly for any business at all you need to understand what it is you want to achieve out of it. Obviously businesses are designed to be profitable but also in my view they must have a long term positive environmental impact to be truly successful. I guess that is what is driving me, I can see great benefits from a bast fibre perspective in downstream manufacturing in thermo and bio based plastics along with the great properties in hurd for its insulation and absorption capabilities. So, I guess anyone who is looking to get involved in a business, first and foremost they need to understand the business they are getting into, second of all to understand the markets, and what markets they are wanting to enter, and what other outside influences can effect those markets. Third major point is that the person getting involved in the business needs to ask themselves how are they going to get out of this business, a bit of an unusual statement to start with, but in order to start you must know what your end use is, what your limitations are.

P: What are the steps involved with growing hemp, if you decide you want to grow hemp, you know why you want to grow hemp, you have a market for growing hemp, and now you just have to grow it, how would you take that idea to getting the seed in the ground? How would you go about it?
S: Provided you have the market, and you understand what the market requires, and you have the capabilities to deliver a product that suits those market capabilities.
Once you understand the market, then especially for industrial hemp in this country you need to understand the laws associated with that, contact the various departments involved. Department of Primary Industries, and if you are importing seed or various products then AQIS is another contact you need to be aware of. You need to understand what you are growing. If you do not understand what you are growing then chances are if you are contracting out to various growers, and they are depending on an income from growing then you could disappoint them, if you have not understood exactly what you need to understand as far

as that crop is concerned and how it operates in an agricultural environment.

Some of the key points are the legislation, licenses and growers and their capabilities are very important. The seed or germ stock you have to grow from is also very important and understanding what market you are getting into and how you are going to grow that crop to satisfy that market. Irrigation is also important as Australia is a dry climate and we need to understand that in order to grow this crop as it should be it does need to be irrigated, Last point, is harvesting, which is the most important as there is no point growing something if you can't extract the value out of it. To be viable it needs to be reasonably cost equivalent and provide returns similar to alternative crops.

P: What does the farmer need to know to grow industrial hemp compared to any other crop

S: For Industrial hemp, it is all about what the stalk fibre is going to be used for so you need to understand the market and just to give you an idea I am a big supporter of fibre and for growing fibre to me it is important to look at plant to plant densities, row to row densities to ensure what I am growing is a stalk, with diameter of no bigger than your little finger and that you have plant populations between 175 to 200 plants per square meter or 1.75 – 2.00 million per hectare to achieve this. So, I guess the farmer needs to understand what equipment he has, is he/she capable of planting to such densities and providing the nutritional requirements, hemp has similar requirements to maize. So I guess he/she needs to understand whether they need herbicides, insecticides, fertiliser, planting equipment, irrigating methods, harvesting equipment, post harvesting handling equipment.

P: So lets talk about them one at a time as there was a lot of information in there. Seed sowing, growing for fibre is very different than growing for seed or dual crop. How many seeds per hectare? How close do you sow seed? What figures can you give?

S: I will give you a general idea, research and observations have shown that plant row spacing no greater than 100mm is ideal, and plant to plant density spacing is 2.5 to 3cm is considered ideal for fibre.

P: For seed it is a lot less is that correct?

S: If you are looking at planting rates per hectare you need to understand how many seeds per kilogram for that particular variety has and to calibrate seed planting equipment to suit the crop you want to grow. Planning for seed you want to have a not so dense crop as fibre, your plant row spaces are also important and you would want to extend those out to 50-80 cm with a row to row spacing of up to 10 - 20cm.

P: You need to know how many seeds are in a kilogram for seed planting machinery that bases calculations on weight. Is that correct?

S: Yes, and you also need to know the germination of that seed, if it is at 75% you need to account for that and compensate for that at kilograms per hectare that you are wanting to sow to get the optimum amount of seeds germinating

P: How do you test the germination rate:

S: You can send away to various companies to tell you that or you can do it yourself, by getting a saucer or some other vessel put tissue paper in the bottom and soak the seeds in water and record the amount of time it takes to get them to germinate. It is a rough way of doing it, but if your resources are limited it is possible.

P: I guess the seed sowing rates for a dual crop are more in the middle of a fibre and seed crop, or is it more like a seed crop.
S: It is more like a seed crop, row densities can be brought down to between 30-50cm and plant to plant densities can be brought down to about 5-15cm

P: What are pros and cons of growing a dual crop? Why wouldn't you grow for both?
S: The biggest problem from a fibre perspective is that you are producing a stem which is quite thick and the worse part about growing from a fibre perspective is that the glues within the fibres have hardened, and they have effectively hardened past the ideal point so the extraction of those fibres is harder. The bast to hurd ratio is much lower; the bast is what you are wanting; so effectively you have a fibre stalk that is up to 2 cm whereas what you are really wanting is a fibre diameter of .5cm or less. There are advantages in that you are getting seed to sell along with the crop, but trials in Europe have shown the fibre extraction process to be much more difficult and also the extraction of that fibre and bast is much lower.

P: So, I guess what you are saying is if you are considering growing a dual crop the only reason you would consider doing that is if you needed the whole stalk. If you wanted to separate the bast and the hurd then it makes sense to just grow a fibre crop, if you want seed just grow seed crop.

S: Yes

P: And I guess there is no reason why you couldn't grow a seed crop next to a fibre crop you just need to change the sowing rates?
S: Absolutely

P: It's just about the market and what the market is demanding of you?
S: No, but this is where I believe a lot of people come unstuck, trying to produce industrial hemp because they have not understood the markets. In order to understand the markets, you need to have a market. A lot of people get excited about hemp, but to me hemp is just another agricultural commodity that provides an incredible benefit not only to agriculture and the soils, but also to manufacturing and industry.

P: Crop nutrients? Is there a particular ideal soil that is used for growing hemp?
S: It comes back to understanding the crop. Hemp has a very long tap root which means it can be advantageous for clay soils however my observations and trials have concluded that the best type of soils for fibre hemp is a free draining sandy/clay loam soils that allows uninhibited growth and extraction of nutrients and moisture

P: Is irrigation important in the beginning, in the middle, at the end or all?
S: For all stages in growth however, Irrigation is also critical at the post harvesting time, reason being that Australia has a generally harsh dry summer. In order to maximize this stalks extraction of fibre, it needs to be retted. Retting is

simply a term that is given to the rotting of the glues that hold the fibres together - the lignin's and pectin's. Irrigation or rain is needed to start this process. Whilst it is very important to grow the crop to its maximum capabilities, it's also very important to have an irrigation method that can be supplied post harvest that can assist in this retting process. Several people in Australia have tried flood irrigating, bearing in mind that when you are flood irrigating any crop it's effectively water logging the crop and inhibiting its full growth potential and in some cases it sets the crop back to the point where that water has to be taken away from it and it allows the plant to breathe again. My preferred method is overhead irrigation which is central pivot or lateral irrigation which mimics rain and is delivered with overhead structures. You can control how much you are putting on per hectare. On the other end of the spectrum you can control where that water droplet goes to assist in the retting process. Overhead irrigation method with water droplets that can be controlled is very important.

P: How much water do you need to irrigate? Its been known that hemp doesn't require so much water?
S: That is true. I guess the issue is how much rain you are going to get into your crop while it is growing, how much sub soil moisture you have stored, what the water holding capacity is of those particular soils. Now taking all that away and working on the basis that you are not going to get any rainfall pre and post crop and you would be working on 3-4 megalitres per hectare. To give you an idea, this would be roughly less than half of what is used in the production of maize or cotton.

P: When is the best time to irrigate?

S: In order for hemp to germinate effectively, ideally you would plant into a dry seed bed and irrigate up, your first irrigation might be 25-50mm per hectare, and then hope you get some rain. Obviously rainfall is a better alternative given that rain drops fixate nitrogen as it is falling and that benefits the crop. If you had to irrigate on an as needed basis you would be monitoring your crop and irrigate accordingly. At first you might give 25-50mm irrigation, then 6-8 weeks later then same again when you have canopy closure, and then as needed as the growth rates dictate. There is plenty of equipment available that can monitor sub-soil moisture and crop usage.

P: While the crop is growing, it has been said that hemp doesn't require herbicides, pesticides and fertilizer. I know that is not always the case.
S: I guess if you look at the fertilizer requirements, there has been a lot of talk that hemp doesn't require fertilizer. That is not true if you are going to grow any crop to its full potential then like you and me the plants need to be fed. You need to understand the nutrients in the soil before planting as over fertilizing industrial hemp can sometimes create a weak stem and in those cases the amount of nitrogen may cause the stems to turn yellow and lodge which makes it difficult to harvest. The NPK ratio for hemp, again it comes down to what market you are growing for and what's in the soil, anywhere between 120-140 N, 30-45P, 35-60 K for fibre crop, seed or dual crop 140-180N, 80-100 P, 80-120K

P: What about herbicides and pesticides?
S: Fibre hemp - unless you have poor germination (bare patches in crop, weeds will grow), you should expect good

germination that forms a near full canopy within 5-6 weeks, and generally the weeds that have germinated with the hemp are shaded out and stunted. Given a configuration of growing a seed crop the spacing is much greater and the addition of herbicides could be required just to ensure you are taking away any weed competition from the hemp. Fibre hemp does not need any insecticides, you will generally harvest before any seed sets. If any insects attack the leaf crop after 5-6 weeks, let them do it, it won't do any damage to the fibre. As far as the seed crop is concerned, insects can be a problem, the worst case I have seen is heliothis and rough boll worms drilling into the stem and growing tips itself and causing the plant to tip out and grow two heads delaying maturity of that crop which creates problems at harvest time with heads having different seed moisture content and maturity. That is a problem when it comes to storage. It needs to be monitored.

P: How would you respond to someone wanting to grow and certify hemp organically or include as a companion plant?
S: I recently learned 85% of the hemp grown in China is used as a companion crop for vegetables; they are growing industrial hemp around their vegetable fields to assist in repelling insects trying to eat their vegetables. Organic – you need to be sure again the market demands organic. Hemp seeds are a good option. At harvest time your yields maybe lower than conventional crops through insect pressure. The extra income may pay for this.
My experience in Germany is that the organic hemp crops I saw there had more insects and grubs than any other seed crop I have ever seen and I have worked over many

different crops. The yield penalty will of course affect the growers back pocket and must be accounted for.

P Once we have grown our crop, when is the ideal time to harvest for any of the three types of hemp crops, worldwide?

S Ok, so lets start with fibre hemp – if you want the absolute best quality fibre possible you will need to harvest the crop at, in my view, first site of male flower, or within 10 days of that period. That is when the highest quality fibre is present AND the glue that holds the fibres together is at its most weakest. If you let that crop go any longer it makes those glues harden and the retting process will need to be extended to break down those fibres. Also, the amount of useable fibre you can extract in that fibre scenario is much better than if you grew a dual purpose or seed crop.

With seed harvesting, obviously, the seed moisture content is very important. Hemp is an oil seed and can prove difficult to store. You want to harvest it when the seed moisture content is somewhere between 12 and no more than 18%. Once it is harvested and graded for all the insects, green leaf and other material, that seed will still be brought down to a moisture content of between 8 and 10% to make sure it will be viable to store.

P What is the viability of different size crops, 1ha or 50ha or 500ha – how does that affect your business?

S If you are going to start with 1ha then you are not going to want to import a machine that automatically harvests for 1/4million$. A simple brush cutter or even a sickle cutter on the side of a tractor is more than enough for a fibre crop.

For a seed crop, you generally need larger hectares. Unless you were to buy a very cheap combine and modified that combine it is not really a viable alternative to grow 1ha. You need to understand the commercial side of the harvesting and make sure it is done as economical as possible.

As far as harvesting machinery for fibre, there are lots of machines on the market, and I have reviewed most of them and I believe the hemp flax method is the most efficient and the best for fibre growing. It is simply a modified Kemper forage harvester. When I say modified I mean the choke or cutting technique is slowed down and also some blades removed to ensure the cut fibre stalk length is up to 60cm or if not, a fraction smaller This allows for good throughput. This will produce a cut stalk fibre that is more than able to be decorticated once that product has retted and dried down enough. (ie. What the market wants).

How the machine cuts the stalk, lots of people have tried the sickle method. It comes back to understanding the market and knowing when you need to harvest that crop. If you let hemp mature too much of the lignin will start to bind the fibre and hurd together. That becomes a problem not only in harvesting but also downstream decortication and uses.

A seed crop is similar to harvesting sorghum or pretty much any other coarse grain. There are some modifications to be made inside that header. This is to stop the splitting of the seed. It is a matter of machine set-up. Ensuring the concaves are wound out to allow plenty of room so the heads can go through without splitting the seed, whilst not letting too much seed pass over the straw walker. It's a fine line with machine set-up.

These are the biggest secrets of the industry! I am giving you all the things to be great successful competitor!

P That's great – we need more competition in this market, we need to all grow together.

S Yes, I agree, There is a big need for much more bast fibre than is available today. More market acceptance.

P It takes time to setup a business. I am hoping others will learn from our experiences and keep in contact to get all the updates so everything is relevant and real.

P What about infield decortication?

S At this point, I don't recommend that, as for the farmer to extract maximum yield and returns; the farmer wants to get as much stalk off the ground as he can as he gets paid on a per tonne basis. Infield decortication – well, I haven't seen a method yet that is affective without large losses of hurd. And I believe you need that hurd to make up the gross margins and viability of your enterprise.

P Historically hemp is harvested infield, is that because of cheap labour?

S Yes! The only reason. If you are growing 1ha or something, then that is fine if you have the time.

P What's the next stage and how do you store the product once it is harvested. Do you bale hemp?

S There is a couple of methods here. For the first 7-10 days the crop needs to lie down and lose its moisture. The green leafy material breaks down, eventually to dust and the smaller branches from the stem will also break down and return to the soil as organic matter which is very beneficial for the forthcoming crops. After 7-10 days a hay rake is used to turn the crop over to ensure an even ret and dry down. This vigorous turning will knock additional leaves and branches off and this will leave a windrow of hemp stalk fibre to be able to continue its retting that can be accessible to baling.

If you want to use a pick-up front to bring it into a bol buggy to put it into a module; which is similar to what the cotton industry use to transport their lint.

Preferably for me is a large square bale. Again, this is CRITICAL, what ever is preferred by your market and the opening mechanism employed at the decortication factory. Whatever way you handle the crop post harvest needs to correspond with whatever opening method you have at the decortication factory, at the mill.

What the through-put capacity you have to process at the mill is a critical part of this.

P So, retting, or leaving the crop on the field is like rotting. To separate the fibre from the hurd. Is that important time for wet weather?

S Yes, you NEED it wet to start the enzyme process to begin retting. If, after 7-10 days you have not had rainfall on that crop you will need overhead irrigation to start this enzyme process. If you don't get rain, then the stalk will end up as a 'sun retted' product, basically bleached stalk only. If you try and decorticate that it produces a very brittle fibre and often turns to dust in which case, there are very low proportions of fibre (less than 5%). However, the quality yield of the hurd will be exceptional. It will be white and attractive; however that is not where the money is. The money is in the bast fibre. If you are in it for the fibre, then degrees of retting are critical to the extraction of the bast fibres.

P What more can you share more about the retting process?

S The 7-10 day period depends on sunlight/ heat and lack thereof. The idea is to break down leaf and branches – you don't want to be baling those. 50-60cm cut retted fibre and hurd is all you want. Nothing else. Prior to baling or using the module method, the stalk moisture should be 10-12% to prevent any spontaneous combustion occurring in storage.

P What else?
S: Transport costs and efficiencies, and how much you can store on a trailer – round bales versus square bales; to maximize your returns for logistics also need to be considered. Speak with your local freight company to get sizes and work with them before you decide. Maybe your purchaser has preferences, again – check what the decortication factory wants.

P What about seed harvesting – using a regular header.
S Yes. After harvesting, I would grade the seed – ie. Taking whole seed away from the rubbish accumulated from the harvesting. This is usually done mechanically using various size screens. Different sized screens are important. You only want one quality of seed. The white non-viable seed is of no use. Check moisture content now. If it requires further drying put the seed in a silo that has a drying fan to get it to 8-12%, ideally low as possible. Then store in silo or 1 tonne or smaller bag, depending on what market you want sell into.

P In regards to the markets you recommend – what are they for fibre ? small and larger uses? How could a farmer up value his crop?
S The farmer may up value by ensuring he has a well-retted stalk. Most companies are willing to pay a little more

for a well retted stalk. They are generally able to extract greater fibre yields and stalk through-put. For niche markets, I don't really know… I guess and if you didn't have a decortication facility maybe you could look at the garden mulch market, you could additionally cut down those stems to a 1-2" arrangement and bale those into small bales, you could sell them into the mulch market.

P Yes, I have seen this product in small 15kg bags being sold in Australia for $18, and they sold out.
S Yes, stalk hemp fibre makes for excellent mulch as the fibres hold the material in place and they don't blow away. It also provides excellent cover against moisture loss and the breakdown over time of the hurd and fibre creates additional organic matter for the soils. It creates a very healthy living environment for micro-organisms.

P How is that compared to other fibres in the mulch market?
S In the same market there are other products such as chickpeas, Lucerne, sugar cane leaf etc. and the retail price is comparable $15-$20 per bale.

P And on a larger scale?
S Yes it's possible. Anything is possible…

P Well if you do then you know your market and have someone to guide you, so if you don't have one of these facilities available to you?
S I will go back to my previous method of mulching the whole stem. Very important it does not have seed in it. If anyone has a germinating plant in their garden from the mulch then obviously questions can be asked. Its best to

ensure the harvesting commences at the first site of male flower for this mulch market.

P As a hemp processor, what is your relationship be with a farmer?
S For those who are processing fibre hemp stalks, it is very important to have a good relationship with your farmers. They need an income too from the hemp they are growing or otherwise they will grow something else on that land. These farmers are generally paid per tonne for what they deliver to the factory location. Prices paid may vary due to the quality of stalk that is being delivered and how well the stalk is retted. Farmers are a very important part of making this industry a success it deserves.

P If you had a secret to give for a hemp grower, what would it be about?
S The secret is RETTING. Most farmers I know are very innovative; they want to grow the best of anything they set their minds to and off course, reap the maximum returns possible. Once they understand how what they produce assists the down stream processing and end uses they constantly strive to achieve this. To get the most and best quality of fibre, it all comes down to the retting process.

P So how do they improve retting?
S Hope for rain after harvest so you don't have to pay for water. It is market dependent again. If you want to process fibre and do it easily, then retting is key.

P Where do people fail in this area?
S Under-retting or stalks being green. This makes it very difficult to extract fibre from hurd, to decorticate. It is

sometimes impossible to process and store. The lignin is a strong binder between the fibre and hurd after harvesting. You can still get slithers of hurd in the fibre after the decortication process and this is the last thing the market wants.

P What are the consequences of this?
S A market that is not happy with the fibre you have delivered and they have paid for. They will need to source other fibre to continue or the decortication factory needs to reprocess or give them a discount on those bales of fibre.

P So how do people stay on top of that.
S By ensuring the stalk fibres is well retted and employing the right irrigation methods, such as the overhead irrigation system we spoke about earlier. In field is the only way to do this.
Most other industries do not want rain at the harvesting time, however with fibre hemp that is opposite.

P So is this overhead irrigation equipment available only if you are growing hundreds of hectares?
S No, this method is available down to 1 ha and up to well, if the farmer provides the design of where he wants to irrigate, irrigation companies will generally design the most efficient system for him.

P what are the problems with pond retting.
S The water is likely to become quite putrid and you would not want that to get into any local water supply. This method is generally only employed in developing countries like China and India for the textile industry. If you diluted the retted water perhaps it could be used to irrigate another

crop. If it is like pasty glue you would not want to use it for anything like that. It's not practical or legal for this in Australia as far as I am aware.

P From your experience, what would you consider the smallest crop worth growing for a decent income.
S Depending on what the farmer currently grows. If he is a vegetable grower and has 10ha and wants $3000 hectare, then hemp is not for him. If a maize, cotton or sorghum grower and he gets $800 hectare and has the right equipment then I guess hemp could fit into his rotations.

P Would you recommend trying growing industrial hemp to all farmers?
S Sure, if you have a market. But don't grow it for the feel good factor unless you have plenty of time and money; first make sure there is a valid use and market demand.

P You are based in Victoria, Australia. Does it make sense growing anywhere in Australia to supply to you?
S If they are in Western Australia then no, the transport costs are prohibitive. However, if they are growing in VIC, NSW or Queensland then the possibility exists provided the growers pay for the transport.

P Anything else?
S I don't take lightly to anyone having motives other than growing industrial hemp for fibre, hurd or seed. If anyone is trying to grow a drug crop then I will not support them in any way. We are creating a legitimate industry here and will report anyone doing anything but the right thing.

P Have you seen anyone do this?

S I have seen fields with hundreds of square metres of heads taken away. Don't tell me that person(s) did not have an ulterior motive in mind.

P Don't try that at home.
S Yes correct, licensed legitimate growers only.

P Thank-you for your time. Are you available to work with us on our mentoring/consultancy program.
S Sure, as long as the people are serious, we will help them!
Don't forget anyone setting up any business needs an exit strategy. You may have a good idea where your business is going but do consider what synergistic partners you may work with or what multi-nationals may want access to a developed business. You may get bigger or sell all or parts of the business. You may take on management or investor buy-in or buy-outs. Different things will suit different people. There will always be an end point – It is just about considering the options in advance and planning for those.

P Great, I have experienced the need for exit strategy at the beginning and fully agree.
Thank-you for your overview of this great industry at this exciting time. We look forward to growing with you in hemp!

Shaun Bailey has plans in place to be a hemp processor in Victoria, Queensland. Contact him via www.TheHempConsultant.com

Cultivation of Industrial Hemp – General Overview
Adapted text from the great work of Julia DesBrosses and Lisa Jackson

This information is a guide only. Please consider all the information in this book as suggestions only, and take advice from your contractor or a local farmer. Local conditions may vary. The following information is based upon Australian conditions, however the data and advice is taken from growing groups, farmers and associations around the world and you can obviously adapt as you require.

Hemp
Hemp (from Old English *hænep*) is the name of the soft, durable fibre that is cultivated from plants of the *Cannabis* genus, cultivated for commercial use. Not to be mistaken with Abaca or 'Manila Hemp', a relative of the banana plant which once replaced hemp's use for rope.

Soils
Hemp will show higher yields in higher quality soils, with sufficient readily available nutrients, favorable water balance and good water permeability.
The ideal soil acidity is between 5.8 and 6.0 pH.
Very rich black mollisols, brown rendzina and brown steppe soils have favorable water balance, good water permeability and an excellent nutrient-accumulation potential.
Hemp may react poorly to residual herbicides in soil, however with time it should be possible to develop a reasonable yield of hemp on soils previously damaged by

chemical usage, helping to improve soil health, and supply industrial inputs for building products or paper, rather than as a food crop.

Nutrients

Nitrogen is considered the most important nutrient for hemp, which needs adequate readily available nitrogen throughout the entire vegetative period to achieve high yields. Including leguminous crops in rotation and addition of natural organic fertilizers if necessary can provide this. Excess N can result in reduced fibre quality and quantity. Hemp is a nitrophilic crop, irrigated crops using in excess of 200 units of Nitrogen, 120 units of Potassium and 40 units of Phosphorus.Hemp requires adequate Calcium and therefore pH should be rectified by liming if acidity limits the availability of any of these nutrients

Phosphorous and potassium are also quite important relating to elasticity and tensile strength of fibre cells or bundles and fibre quality respectively.

Mulches, seaweeds, fly ash, bird and animal manures, comfrey, rock dusts, treated waste water, lime, composite, and rotational crop choice, can all help improve the nutrient qualities of soils.

Hemp requires less than 1/3rd of the nitrogen and less than ½ of the phosphoric acid that does cotton.

Hemp removes minimal ingredients permanently from the soil in comparison to wheat, corn, tobacco and such like.

Pre-crop

Legumes, clovers, lupins will enhance nitrogen levels and organic matter content of soils

Companion Crops

Interplanting hemp with mixed tree species will provide wind protection, improve water balance and can themselves be utilized as valuable crops. In Australia, using plants such as native Acacias can also provide mulch high in nitrogen

Hemp can be grown on the same land more than once, however like any crop – rotation is preferred and recommended.

Soil Preparation

Tillage methods that retain precipitation, incorporate the nutrients into the soil, sustain porosity and keep a smooth surface are recommended

Yeomans type ploughing can improve compacted soils, aerating and de-compacting soils whilst protecting soil biological processes.

Crops can be grown with no-tillage methods such as espoused in the 'One Straw Revolution', by Matsuoba Fukuoka, and should be applicable to hemp production in the long term.

Hemp is able to extract heavy metal from the soil in amounts higher than many other agricultural crops. This has been shown by the 'mop cropper' Dr Keith Bolton in Australia. Gross primary biomass increments up to 23 t/ha and CO_2 sequestration range between 7.6 tC/ha and 11.5 tC/ha.

Temperature and irrigation
The range for optimal growth is between 19 and 25°c (66°-77°F).
50-70 cm of precipitation are recommended for good plant growth and high yields, with 25-30 cm of that being during the vegetative period, or other adequate water, such as a water table within a metre of the surface. However hemp has shown reasonable yields in dry land farming trials. If irrigation is used it is important to avoid flood irrigation on early seedlings.

Seeds
Fresh, clean, bright, plump glossy seed that is one year old is ideal. Test for fertility rates if 2 years or more old.

Cultivars

Different varieties of hemp seed provide different properties of hemp – so know your use first and check with your seed supplier if the variety you have requested is appropriate. Suppliers of hemp seed are available via www.hemp.co.uk Certified low THC hemp seed is currently available from Canada, Eastern and Western Europe, China, Australia and is currently under development in the United States The hemp growth cycle is regulated by day length and this must be considered when selecting appropriate seed. A Northern European or Canadian cultivar will mature faster closer to the Equator, providing less time for plant growth, making Southern European or Chinese varieties more advantageous in terms of growth cycles. However, cultivars will adapt to regional environments over time. Soil type will also influence strain selection, as well as the desire for fibre or seed quality.

In Australia there are no limits to what varieties you use, except for the THC limits of .35% in stem,leaf and 50 ppm in seed oil.

The cultivars that have demonstrated as growing well in Tasmania are Kompolti, Futura, Zolo, Anka, Fasarmo, CHG, CHA, USO 14, USO 30, Finola, Charlamagna.

As far as I am aware another variety, Finola is the shortest, and earliest to bloom, of any variety of industrial hemp, and is dioecious, with distinct male and female plants. The crop typically begins to flower at 25-30 days after sowing, with males flowers being the easiest to see with the unaided eye, and mature females do not branch significantly during their subsequent development, even when standing alone.

Go to http://www.finola.com/FinolaDevelopment gif.pdf to download a 2.6 MB pdf that shows the development of FINOLA in pictures, with special emphasis on typical morphologic features of males and females, according to days after sowing. FINOLA produces abundant grain at high latitude (e.g., 62 N), where most other varieties of hemp do not even set seed. In the Northern Hemisphere it is typically planted in May and harvested about 135 days after planting. FINOLA has been developed with traditional methods. It is NOT a product of GM technology!

FINOLA supports natural biodiversity, where ever it is grown; from honey bees and other insects that take pollen from mature male plants in mid-summer, to migratory song birds that fatten up on mature seeds during harvest time, and even the falcons, hawks and owls that come to feed at leisure on smaller birds and field rodents..

Planting
Hemp in the southern hemisphere temperate regions is usually sown between September to November. In the northern hemisphere hemp is generally sown in the spring – from March to May.
A fertile astrological sign, during the first or second quarter moon is recommended
An exact date is chosen with all these factors in mind, including precipitation.

Sow Rate
Fibre crop approximately 80 kg/Ha
Seed crop approximately 40 kg/Ha
Or 100-200 plants/m^2

Planting at the higher density results in minimal branching, improves the quality bast fibre for textile use, almost complete ground cover and weed suppression. Wider spacing of plants allows for more branching and higher seed yields.

Sow Method

Regularly spaced plantings assist uniformity of crop qualities. Seed depth 2-5 cm, with uniformity preferred. Deeper for light soils.
Normal combine seeder can be used.
Both broadcast and drill sowing have been used successfully.

Irrigation

Only if dry first few weeks or general very low rainfall. Avoid flooding young crop. Use of treated waste water for irrigation will also increase soil nitrogen levels (although food standards need to be followed for a crop intended for human consumption). Ensuring adequate irrigation is often well rewarded.

Pests

In hemp crops in Australia, many pests have been recorded but few have warranted control. In fibre crops, Heliothis (Helicoverpa spp.), Red Shouldered leaf beetles (Monolepta australis), Green Vegie Bug (Nezaria viridula), Jassid (Batracomorphus angustatus) and Lucerne Flea (Sminthurus viridis) have been recorded. Fungal attack has caused minor occurrences of plant death in trials in Queensland and New South Wales and has been identified as species of Sclerotinia and Sclerotium, or White Mould.

The infection has been more prevalent in clay soils or where frequent watering occur, creating a wet-dry cycle which encourages the disease. In no cases of fibre crops were these pests or diseases present in large numbers or at economically damaging levels. Root knot nematodes (Meloidogyne spp.) and other nematodes have been identified in the root systems of hemp in cropping soils where nematodes are known to be a problem (e.g. sugarcane areas). In some cases, infection with nematodes is thought to be the cause of considerably reduced plant yields.

In the southern hemisphere Fungi is hemp's most common type of pathogen. Yellow leaf spot, grey mould, hemp canker, downy mildew, fusarium stem canker and fusarium wilt are the most well known. Meloidogne haplii is a nematode worth noting, while parasitic plants include dodder and broom-rape. Viral organisms such as alfalfa mosaic virus, arabis mosaic virus, cucumber mosaic virus, hem mosaic virus and hemp streak virus may be infected via insects. Hemp's THC levels usually inhibit most viruses. Spider mites and the hemp russet mite are known to attack. Birds can be a pest, at the early stages of germination and particularly to seed crops.

Lastly, the human pest is prevalent, believing the industrial hemp crop is actually a drug marijuana crop. Licenses usually require locations that avoid this, however the farmer may benefit from the use of signage to this effect.

Seed Storage

Wet or green seed needs to by dried soon after harvesting, preferably within the first 24 hours, and stored with a moisture level between 9-10%, to preserve viability.

Useful dessicants might include - word ash, neem leaves, etc.

Yield

Growth relates to levels of photosynthetically active radiation including heat.

Results of Victorian and NSW hemp trials have shown yields of 7-14 ton dry stem/Ha, plant height can easily reach three meters.

Overseas seed crops have been reported to readily yield 500 – 1000 kg seed/Ha, with higher seed yields being reported from newer cultivar

Harvesting

Harvesting is 3-4 months. Fibre hemp is ready before seed hemp. If being used for textiles the plants should be harvested a little earlier – at the first appearance of the indications of bloom upon the male stalks.

Smallholder plots are usually harvested by hand. The plants are cut at 2 to 3 cm above the soil and left on the ground to dry. Traditionally hemp was gathered in stooks and leaned in a 'tipi' like structure to air dry. Mechanical harvesting is now common, using specially adapted cutter-binders or simpler cutters. One harvesting unit has been made from a specially modified Kemper front with an added billetising unit designed to handle the hemp stalks, even in high yielding paddocks, chopping it into 600 mm lengths ready for infield drying, raking and baling.

The cut hemp is laid in swathes to dry for up to four days. This was traditionally followed by retting, either water retting (the bundled hemp floats in water) or dew retting (the hemp remains on the ground and is affected by the moisture in dew moisture, and by molds and bacterial action). Modern processes use steam and machinery to separate the fibre, a process known as thermo-mechanical pulping.

Processing

It is not the intention of this book to cover the processing of hemp as it is expected the farmer already has a use in mind.

Most uses of hemp require retting as their primary process. However defoliation may become a necessary step. Some times the stalks are left to dry in the field, sometimes it is preferred to ret wet.

Various forms of retting include dew-retting, snow retting, water-retting, stem-retting, chemical-retting and boiling. New promised technologies include infield mechanical decortication, though this technology has not yet been proven (2010). Dew retting is the most popular – this is simply leaving the stalks on the ground and turning occasionally. This is however, considered inferior to water-retting. Details of water-retting maybe available on request. Further technologies suitable for on processing decorticated fibres for the textile industry include Crailar, an enzyme technology that may well revolutionize this particular industry. There is an interview with the Crailar Board of Directors included in my ebook on the textile industry.

Australian Gross Margins 2010
IRRIGATED FIBRE HEMP GROWING GROSS MARGINS

Forecasted Irrigated Fibre Hemp Gross Margins			T per Ha	T per Ha	T per Ha	T per Ha	T per Ha	T per Ha
Shown in $AUD	$ per T		8	8	10	10	12	12
Income	180		1440		1800		2160	
	200			1600		2000		2400
Variable Costs (per Hectare)								
Cultivation	Scarify	$6 HA	6	6	6	6	6	6
Pre-Irrigate	.75 ML/ha	$30 ML	22.5	22.5	22.5	22.5	22.5	22.5
	Fuel	$40 HA	40	40	40	40	40	40
Herbicide	CT	1L @ $4	4	4	4	4	4	4
	Application	$6 HA	6	6	6	6	6	6
Fertiliser	Urea	125kg @ $550 HA	68.75	68.75	68.75	68.75	68.75	68.75
	DAP	150kg @ $550 HA	82.5	82.5	82.5	82.5	82.5	82.5
	Starter Z	60kg @ $600	36	36	36	36	36	36
Planting	Seed	60kg/ha @ $2kg	120	120	120	120	120	120
	Application	$10/ha	10	10	10	10	10	10
1st Irrigation	.75 ML/ha	$30 ML	22.5	22.5	22.5	22.5	22.5	22.5
	Fuel	$40 HA	40	40	40	40	40	40
2nd Irrigation	.75 ML/ha	$30 ML	22.5	22.5	22.5	22.5	22.5	22.5
	Fuel	$40 HA	40	40	40	40	40	40
3rd Irrigation Retting	.50 ML/ha	$30 ML	22.5	22.5	22.5	22.5	22.5	22.5
	Fuel	$40 HA	40	40	40	40	40	40
Harvest	Kemper	$60/HA	60	60	60	60	60	60
	Conditioning	$8/HA	8	8	8	8	8	8
	Pick-up	$15/HA	15	15	15	15	15	15
	Module Making	$50/HA	50	50	50	50	50	50

	Pick-up & Transport	$50/HA	50	50	50	50	50	50
			1440	1600	1800	2000	2160	2400
Variable Costs per HA			$766	$766	$766	$766	$766	$766
Gross Margin per HA			$674	$834	$1,034	$1,234	$1,394	$1,456
Gross Margin per ML	3ML/HA		225	278	345	411	465	485
			Expected Range for Grower income					

Archived Ontario Production Costs, Canada

Exhibit 3 Selected Crop Production Costs in Ontario 1995 ($/Acre)					
Expenses		Grain Corn	Canola	Hemp For Fibre & Hurds	Hemp For Seed
Cash Operating Costs				22.9kg/ac 29.2kg/ac	6.0kg/ac
Seed		36	12	61.8 78.75	16.2
Seed Treatment		1.5			
Fertilizer	Total	58	43	40 40	40
Chemical	Herbicides	32	8	0 0	10
	Insecticides	13	3	0 0	5
	Other				
Machinery Operating	Fuel	12	9.5	12 12	12
	Repair & Maintenance	26	21	26 26	26
Custom Work and Hired Labour		8	6	8 8	8
Crop Insurance Premium		13	7	7 7	7
Revenue Insurance		12	5	5 5	5
Premium					
Utilities		1.65	1.65	1.65 1.65	1.65
Miscellaneous Overhead		2.5	2.5	2.5 2.5	2.5
Building Repair		1.15	1.15	1.15 1.15	1.15
Property Taxes		3.75	3.75	3.75 3.75	3.75
Interest on Operating		8	2.5	8 8	8
Total Cash Operating Costs (A)		228.55	126.05	176.85 193.8	146.25
Non Cash Costs					
Machinery Depreciation		28.75	23.5	28.75 28.75	28.75
Building Depreciation		1.15	1.15	1.15 1.15	1.15
Machinery Investment		17.5	14	17.5 17.5	17.5
Building Investment		1.85	1.85	1.85 1.85	1.85
Land Cost		23	23	23 23	23
Labour and Management		19	19	19 19	19
Total Non-Cash Costs (B)		49.25	40.5	91.25 91.25	91.25
Total Costs (A+B) = (C)		277.8	166.55	268.1 285.05	237.5

Sources: Gordon Reichert, Market Analysis Division, Agriculture and Agri-Food Canada, 1996 Crop Budgets 1995, Publication #60, Ontario Ministry of Agriculture, Food and Rural Affairs Expected Average Yields, estimates by Ontario Ministry of Agriculture, Food and Rural Affairs

back to hemp reports

Characteristics of Hemp & Flax

Characteristics of hemp and flax

	Flax	Hemp
Name	Linum usitatissimum	Cannabis sativa
Climatic regions	Temperate and sub-tropical	Temperate and sub-tropical
Fibre length (ultimates) mm	20 – 23	9 – 20
Fibre diameter (μm)	22	22
Cellulose (%)	56 – 64	67
Straw yield (tonnes/ha)	2.5 – 4.0	5.0 – 7.0
Fibre yield	20%	20%

Market
Specialty Paper
Cigarette paper
Tea bags
Low value non-wovens
Carpet backing
Automotive Insulation
Beds
Medium value nonwovens
Biodegradable geo-textiles
Automotive composites
High Value Non-wovens
Insulation
Composites
Disposable surgical sheets
Textiles

www.hemp.co.uk

European Hemp Seed Varieties

Hemp			
Variety	Origin	THC (%)	
Carmagnola	Italy	NA	NA
CS	Italy	NA	NA
Delta-Llosa	Spain	NA	NA
Delta-405	Spain	NA	NA
Epsilon 68	NA	NA	NA
Fedora 19	France	0.26	Monoecious
Fedrina 74	France	0.25	Monoecious
Felina 34	France	0.15	Monoecious
Ferimon	France	0.17	Monoecious
Fibranova	Italy	NA	Dioecious
Fibrimon 24	France	0.26	Monoecious
Fibrimon 56	France	0.2-0.56	Monoecious
Futura	France	0.15-0.32	Monoecious
Santhica 23	NA	NA	NA

Industrial Hemp Production in Canada

Prepared by: G. Nabi Chaudhary Economics Branch, AARD,
February 2, 2010

Industrial hemp (Cannabis sativa) is one of the oldest
cultivated plants in the world. The species was banned in
North America in late 1930s because its leaves and flowers
contained a hallucinogenic drug known as delta-9
tetrahydrocannabinol (THC). It was banned internationally
in 1961 under the United Nations' Single Convention on
Narcotic Drugs. Hemp does suffer from the "snicker factor",
largely because of its hippy-dippy image and close
association with marijuana, its conscious-altering cousin.

Effective March 12, 1998, the commercial production
(including cultivation) of industrial hemp is now permitted in
Canada, under licenses and authorization, issued by Health
Canada. This action was prompted by several years of field
research and lobbying by the agricultural and business
community. Prior to 1998, there were only a handful of
licenses issued to grow industrial hemp in Canada. In 1998,
the first year after Health Canada opened up the licensing
process, 241 licenses were issued. These licensees grew
almost 2 370 hectares (5,857 acres) of hemp for industrial
use. In 1999, the number of applications to grow hemp
jumped dramatically to 545 with the area of hemp
production increasing six-fold to nearly 14 031 hectares
(34,657 acres). It looked as though the industrial hemp was
well on its way to becoming the "Cinderella" crop in
Canada. However, events in the summer of 1999, i.e., the
demise of the perspective hemp processing company in
Manitoba, changed the outlook for hemp production in
Canada.   The number of licensees decreased by over 53

percent to 255 and area by almost 63 percent to 5 487 hectares (13,553 acres) in 2000. In 2001, industrial hemp acreage further decreased very dramatically to 1 316 hectares (3,250 acres). In 2002, production of industrial hemp showed an increase of 16 percent to 1 530 hectares (3,778 acres). Then in 2003, the area licensed to produce industrial hemp again increased by almost 79 percent to 2 733 hectares (6,750 acres) but this was still nowhere near the 1999 level (See Table below). It appears that interest in producing industrial hemp is again coming back. In 2004, area licensed for industrial hemp production increased by 28 percent over in 2003 to 3 531 hectares (8,721 acres). In 2005, area licensed for hemp production in Canada increased almost three-folds to 9 725 hectares (24,021 acres).

The largest increases in hemp production area were in Manitoba and Saskatchewan. Area under hemp production increased to its highest level in 2006 at 19 458 hectares (48,060 acres) almost double than in 2005. Prairie Provinces again lead the country in hemp production with almost 97 percent of hemp area. Manitoba had 10 705 hectares (26,442 acres) of hemp followed by Saskatchewan at 6 025 hectares (14,882 acres) and Alberta at 2 103 hectares (5,194 acres). Area under hemp decreased by about 68 per cent in 2007, primarily due to lack of processing facilities for hemp fiber and stock. In 2008, area licensed for commercial hemp production in Canada further decreased by almost 47 percent to 3 259 hectares (8,050 acres). Total number of licenses issued by Health Canada was 85 in 2008, a significant decrease over the last few years.

In 2009, area licensed for hemp production increased by 72 percent across Canada over in 2008, i.e., from 3 259 hectares (8,050 acres) to 5 602 hectares (13,837 acres). Major increases in area were again on the Prairie Provinces lead by Manitoba (145%) and Saskatchewan (34%). Area under hemp production in Alberta increased by 200 hectares (524 acres) over in 2008. Only province to report decrease in hemp area in 2009 was Quebec from 134 hectares (331 acres) in 2008 to 92 hectares (227 acres) in 2009. In British Columbia, area for hemp production increased from five (5) hectares in 2008 to 84 hectares in 2009. Similarly, area in Ontario increased from mere eight (8) hectares in 2008 to 132 hectares in 2009.

Table 1 below provides data on commercial hemp production in Alberta and Canada from 1998 to 2009. Tables 2 and 3 provide hemp production in Canada by provinces from 1998 to 2009 in hectares and acres. A figure below shows hemp production trend in Canada from 1998 to 2009. The industrial hemp production received a lot of attention in the early years. Advocates of hemp production painted a rather rosy picture for growth potential. However, the sudden demise of Consolidated Growers and Processors (CGP) Inc. of California left a large number of hemp growers in Manitoba sitting with a huge crop and nowhere to market it. This company was largely responsible for the rapid increase in acres in 1999 and the fallout in 2000. The company created a lot of interest and hype for hemp among producers, particularly in Manitoba. The CGP contracted an estimated 40 per cent of the total industrial hemp area licensed in Canada in 1999. However, the company went into receivership after failing to meet contractual obligations. This left the hemp producers with a huge surplus of hemp seed and fiber hanging over the market. This surplus was stored in warehouses and farmers' bins, awaiting bankruptcy settlement. A considerable portion of the hemp crop did not get sold and producers had to absorb the losses. Thus, the negative events of 1999 have brought a lot of skepticism and fear for the future growth potential of hemp industry in Canada. However, the downturn in hemp cultivation during the last three –four years is buoyed by a steady increase in the processing of hemp, and the development of many small businesses engaged in developing new products and marketing of these products.

In Alberta, work is well underway at Alberta Research Council (ARC) and Alberta Agriculture and Rural Development (AARD) to evaluate hemp as a potential source of producing pulp and fiber. Currently, there are many Canadian companies – including Hempola Valley Farms; Fresh Hemp Foods; Ruths Hemp Foods; HMF Sales and Marketing; Hemp Oil Canada; Cool Hemp; Natures Path; However; among others – working with hemp food. Many of these companies have strong regional distribution but there is no clear national leader yet. All of these companies are involved in the hemp seed market and are producing a wide range of products. These are snack foods, hemp meal and flour, edible oil, shampoo and conditioners, moisturizers, commercial oil paints, beer and aromatherapy and cosmetic products. Most of the companies are reporting good growth. Another trend worth noting is that much of the hemp food industry has switched to certified organic production because of strong demand. A few industry experts estimate that around 1/3 of Canadian hemp seed production is certified organic.

Another interesting development is that a few years ago the National Research Council Canada (NRC) entered into collaboration with Hemptown Clothing Inc., a manufacturer of hemp clothing that has promoted the idea of using hemp fabric for the uniforms of Canada's 2010 Olympic team. Under this partnership, Hemptown has been working with the NRC Institute for Biological Sciences (NRC-IBS) to commercialize NRC developed enzyme technology for processing hemp fabric (enzymes are used widely in industrial applications for everything from pulp bleaching to meat tenderizers). The technology promises dramatically improved fiber quality (softer, whiter fabric) using environmentally friendly methods.

Table 1
History of Commercial Hemp Production in Alberta and Canada, 1998 - 2009

Year	Alberta Hectares	Alberta Acres	Canada Hectares	Canada Acres	% Alberta
1998	38	93	2 371	5,857	1.59
1999	745	1,840	14 031	34,657	5.31
2000	306	756	5 487	13,553	5.58
2001	113	279	1 316	3,250	8.59
2002	123	304	1 530	3,780	8.04
2003	153	379	2 733	6,750	5.61
2004	639	1,577	3 531	8,721	18.09
2005	916	2,262	9 725	24,021	9.42
2006	2 103	5,194	19 458	48,060	10.81
2007	1 455	3,593	6 132	15,145	23.71
2008	582	1,437	3 259	8,050	17.85
2009	782	1,932	5 602	13,837	13.96

Source: Health Canada

Table 2
Hemp Production in Canada, 1998 - 2009 (Hectares)

Year	BC	Alberta	Sask.	Man.	Ontario	Quebec	NB	NS	PEI	Yukon	Canada
1998	72	38	263	606	1 163	24	214	19	0	0	2 400
1999	225	754	3 096	8 889	1 021	86	4	126	4	0	14 205
2000	291	306	1 426	2 902	217	239	1	102	2	0	5 485
2001	96	113	392	472	209	30	0	0	0	4	1 312
2002	200	123	449	597	142	19	0	0	0	0	1 530
2003	7	153	672	1 468	397	13	4	18	0	0	2 733
2004	18	639	1 004	1 655	183	10	4	18	0	0	3 531
2005	0	916	3 429	5 018	251	74	19	18	0	0	9 725
2006	111	2 103	6 025	10 705	398	91	8	18	0	0	19 458
2007	70	1 455	2 293	2 088	40	182	4	0	0	0	6 132
2008	5	582	1 537	993	8	134	0	0	0	0	3 259
2009	84	782	2 061	2 435	132	92	0	0	16	0	5 602

Source: Health Canada

Table 3
Hemp Production in Canada, 1998 - 2009 (Acres)

Year	BC	Alberta	Sask.	Man.	Ontario	Quebec	NB	NS	PEI	Yukon	Canada
1998	178	94	650	1,497	2,873	59	529	47	0	0	5,927
1999	556	1,862	7,640	21,950	2,523	212	10	312	10	0	35,075
2000	719	756	3,522	7,179	535	590	2	252	4	0	13,559
2001	237	279	968	1,165	516	74	0	0	0	10	3,239
2002	495	304	1,110	1,474	351	47	0	0	0	0	3,781
2003	18	379	1,661	3,625	981	32	10	44	0	0	6,750
2004	44	1,577	2,480	4,089	451	26	10	44	0	0	8,721
2005	0	2,263	8,469	12,395	620	182	47	44	0	0	24,021
2006	273	5,194	14,882	26,442	982	224	20	44	0	0	48,060
2007	173	3,593	5,663	5,157	99	450	10	0	0	0	15,145
2008	12	1,437	3,798	2,453	20	331	0	0	0	0	8,050
2009	207	1,932	5,090	6,015	325	228	0	0	39	0	13,837

Source: Health Canada

Hemp Production in Canada (Hectares), 1998-2009

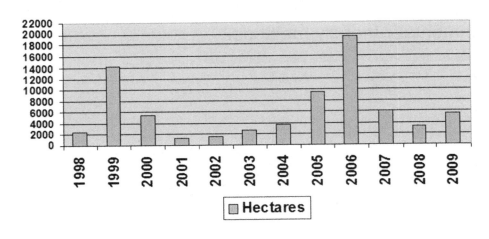

Availability of industrial hemp seed in Australia

The Queensland Government regulations require industrial hemp varieties bred for sale in Australia to be registered with IP Australia before they can become available for approved use. The web address below has a database that anyone can view on what industrial hemp varieties are provisionally protected or registered, you search under the Genus Cannabis:

(GRANTED = fully protected, ACCEPTED = Provisionally protected, yet to be confirmed by replicated trials)
http://www.ipaustralia.gov.au/pbr/index.shtml

Any suitably low THC varieties maybe imported or purchased from a registered licensed seed handler.

Other regulations require that growers obtain an industrial hemp license in order to be able to grow industrial hemp. Growers must have a criminal free record for the past 10 years or they may be refused a license. All blocks have to be approved before use by the industrial hemp Regulator of each State. As yet the protocols for approved seed are not yet finalized but we hope that will be done shortly in Queensland. The Queensland Regulator may allow growers to grow our varieties if the company states that plants produced of the variety grown will not exceed 0.5% Tetra-hydrocannabinol (THC) in the leaves and flowering heads of the plants sampled by the Regulating Body of each State. Licensed growers can import seed that is certified in another country that Australia recognizes as having sufficient regulations in place to supply low THC industrial hemp. An import permit through the Australian Government is required to import seed and has to go through quarantine inspection before release. Quarantine permits also have to be arranged before importation of seed. The export country has to obtain an export permit prior to shipment and have the import documentation from the importer. However, many overseas varieties of industrial hemp are not well adapted to sub-tropical environments and may not grow as tall as they do in their country of origin. Most temperate varieties flower in about 30 days under sub-tropical conditions and this can lead to short plants. However, Queensland bred industrial hemp is reliable under sub-tropical conditions. Visit www.hemp.co.uk for your independent seed supplier.

Why companies require royalties or non propagation agreements

The breeding of industrial hemp is a technical operation and the breeder has to keep the THC content well below the upper limit of 0.5% THC in order to allow for environmental influence such as day length, soil type and other environmental conditions. Stable varieties below 0.2% THC will be reliable and not exceed the THC limit imposed by Government. One Queensland Company is continuing to improve sub-tropical varieties and has two varieties below 0.05% THC. One is a dual-purpose variety and the other a fibre variety. In developing the new varieties from late flowering hybrid varieties at least four years of development is required to obtain uniform plants that can pass the standard for Plant Breeders Rights. The breeder has to justify statistically that the variety is distinct, uniform and stable. A replicated trial is required containing two generations of the candidate variety and one generation of a variety of common knowledge (a variety known to IP Australia or a variety from overseas with some characteristics common to the candidate variety). An examiner from IP Australia visits the trial to verify that the breeder has a statistically sound trial and the claims made that the variety is true to type, distinct and stable verified. This costs the company $1,800.00 per variety or slightly cheaper if more than one variety is registered at a time. The development costs to the company for breeding the varieties we currently own is in excess of a million dollars. The company in order to receive any kind of return for this plant breeding development means that a royalty be paid by the other party growing the variety. Added to the technical obstacles of ensuring the plants are kept uniform, distinct and stable isolation of five kilometres is required from other varieties as industrial hemp is a wind pollinated crop in order to keep the line pure.

Benefits of industrial hemp

Fibre varieties

The outer fibre of industrial hemp contains the strongest known natural fibre. This outer fibre called bast fibre has many uses other than the traditional uses for sail, canvas making and clothing manufacture. It can be used in producing a glassless replacement for fiberglass, is a good insulator for homes. The inner fibre contains shorter more solid fibres called hurds. Hurd can be used in many building products such as light weight but strong hemp boards as apposed to traditional chip board. It will form highly sound proof interior walling and because hurds are composed of hemi-cellulose it can be manufactured into polymers ranging from bio-degradable plastics to almost ceramics that can withstand a blow torch. The hurds can make a highly stable and strong hemp-crete block with a lower Carbon foot print than standard bricks or concrete blocks and hemp-crete blocks weight less than standard materials. The whole stalk is also used in building materials as seen at www.TheHempBuilder.com

Grain varieties and animal feeds

Currently industrial hemp seed is not allowed in Australia as human food although it is legal in many other countries including the United States of America. Our company is vigorously approaching State and Federal Governments to legalize hemp as a human food. Hemp meal that is the product after cold pressing the seed for oil is highly nutritious for stock. It contains essential fatty acids, a full range of amino acids, vitamins, minerals, soluble and insoluble dietary fibre and has a very high protein content in a very tasty and digestible form.

 The oil is also highly nutritious and has been shown to have good skin healing properties. It not only softens skin but helps heal minor wounds and is excellent for people who have skin complaints.

Hemp research and growing in Ukraine

Pavlo Holoborod'ko

Institute of Bast Crops, Hlukhiv, Ukraine

Introduction   Hemp has been grown in Ukraine for centuries. Before the 1950s the area under hemp cultivation in Ukraine exceeded 150,000 ha.

Table 1. Area of hemp production in Ukraine from 1950-1993.

Years	Hemp area (1,000 ha)
1950	15.3
1960	97.4
1970	63.1
1980	31.6
1990	10.2
1993	5.7

Hemp fibre was widely used in the manufacture of technical products, and was used by peasants to make cloth, clothes and household goods. Hemp seeds, after different kinds of processing, and hemp seed oil, were used as food and for technical purposes.   The large-scale cultivation of cheaper cotton, and development of the synthetic fibres industry caused the hemp area in Ukraine, as well as all over the world, to decrease. This decline was also due to the spread of its use as a drug, especially in the southern regions of Ukraine.   In 1994, about 4,000 ha were sown for fibre hemp in Ukraine. Hemp was grown in three zones: the northern zone (Sumy region ~1,000 ha), the forest and steppe zone (Poltava and Cherkassy region ~2,000 ha), and the steppe zone (Dnipropetrovs'k region ~1,000 ha). Hemp fibre is used exclusively to manufacture technical products such as marine and river cordage, ropes, cores for steel cables, twines, technical clothes, etc. Since industrial demand for hemp fiber is not satisfied, and there is a large demand for hemp products, the area under hemp production in Ukraine will increase.

Contemporary history

During 1929-1930 in the Soviet Union large collective farms (kolkhoz) and state farms (sovkhoz) replaced individual peasant farms. Hemp growing was concentrated on collective farms or state farms with 100-500 ha sown. In 1931, the All-Union Scientific and Research Institute of Bast Crops was organized in the town of Hlukhiv to study problems of the cultivation, harvesting, and processing of hemp. The Institute exists now as the Institute of Bast Crops of the Ukrainian Academy of Agrarian Sciences and carries out research on hemp and fiber flax. For more than 60 years the Institute thoroughly investigated the problems of the anatomy, biology, and physiology of hemp plants, researched selection and genetics; developed methods of hemp growing for different soil and climatic zones, developed technologies of harvesting stalks and seeds and primary fiber processing, and designed harvesting equipment.

Ukrainian hemp breeding progressed through two stages. During the first stage, local varieties with stem fiber content of 12-15% long fiber yield were replaced by the dioecious hemp varieties with high fiber content. The varieties US-1, US-6, US-9, Hlukhivska 1, and Hlukhivska 10 were grown in the northern zone, Yuzhna Cherkasska was grown in the forest and steppe zone, and Dniprovs'ka 4, Yuzhna Krasnodars'ka, and Krasnodars'ka 35 were grown in the south of Ukraine and the Northern Caucasus. Due to acclimatization in different zones of southern hemp varieties, and to use of different methods of hybridization and breeding, stem fiber content in these varieties was increased to 22-27%, and in some varieties stem fiber content exceeded 30%.

The second stage of hemp breeding consisted in development of monoecious hemp varieties which could help solve the problems of harvest mechanization. In the early 1960s the hemp variety Bernburgska Odnodomna from Germany was grown. Hybridization of that variety with the dioecious hemp variety US-6 of high fiber content, and subsequent breeding, resulted in 1968 in the high yield monoecious hemp variety USO-1. Later the varieties USO-4, Poltavska Odnodomna 3, and USO-16 were developed. Since the 1980s only monoecious hemp has been grown in Ukraine.

Due to the spread of the use of illicit drugs, many countries imposed limitations, and even made hemp growing illegal. According to the laws of the Soviet Union it was illegal to grow new hemp varieties with tetrahydrocannabinol (THC) content higher than 0.3%. Later the allowable THC content was reduced to 0.25%, and since 1988 it has been reduced to 0.1%. Hemp breeding for low cannabinoid content was preceded by study of cannabinoid combinations, through determining different methods of analysis and diagnostics including express diagnostics, which underlay the methods of breeding hemp varieties with low drug potency. Several generations of varieties with different THC content were developed. At present 5 hemp varieties with low THC content and differing economic indices are being grown in Ukraine.

Table 2   *Agronomic Data for Ukranian Hemp Cultivars*

Varieties	Vegetative Cycles	Yield (t/ha) stalks	Seeds	Stem Fiber Content (% d.w.)	THC content (% d.w.)
USO-31	115-120	8	0.8-1.2	30-32	0.06
USO-14	120-125	8-9	0.8-1.2	30-32	0.16
USO-11	125-130	9-10	0.8-1.0	27-28	0.2
USO-13	140-145	9-10	0.8-1.0	27-28	0.14
Dniprovs'ka Odnodomna	140-150	9-10	0.7-1.0	30-31	0.18

Present techniques

The system of seed growing of monoecious hemp varieties preserves a high level of varietal typicalness. To produce super-elite seeds and elite seeds staminate plants are removed.

Plants in the first reproduction are grown under the conditions of spatial isolation and free cross-pollination and the number of starninate plants does not exceed 5%.

Seeds of the second reproduction are used to grow hemp only for fiber and the number of staminate plants does not exceed 25%.

Table 3. Characterization of stem fiber content in gene bank accessions.

Fiber content (% d.w.)	Number of accessions
10-15%	88
16-20%	125
21-25%	20
26-30%	27
>30%	10

Since 1992, following the proclamation of the independent state of Ukraine, the Institute has been working on the formation of the national gene bank of bast crops. In 1994, 283 hemp accessions (211 dioecious and 72 monoecious) were studied.

The collection was thoroughly investigated for fiber and cannabinoid content, stalk and seed yield, plant height, length of vegetative cycle, and resistance to diseases and pests. The most valuable accessions were introduced as initial material for breeding.

Table 4. Characterization of THC content in gene bank accessions.

THC content (% d.w.)	Number of accessions
0.0-0.5%	6
0.06-0.19%	30
0.20-0.30%	30
0.40-0.50%	35
>0.50%	182

The Institute developed agrotechnical hemp-growing methods for the soil and climatic, organizational, and economic conditions of Ukraine. Hemp is cultivated in special short rotations. In kolkhozes and sovkhozes with large hemp areas, hemp is grown in cereal root crop rotations. Recently an energy-saving system of soil preparation in hemp rotations was developed based on the combination of mold-board plowing and post-plowing tillage.

Fertilizers consisting of nitrogen (N), phosphorous (P), and potassium (K) macro nutrients and boron (B), bromine (Br), copper (Cu), and Zinc (Zn) micro nutrients are applied according to the results of soil diagnostics.

Two hemp-growing technologies are used in Ukraine. The first technology is for the production of fiber and seed. Hemp is sown in wide rows at row width of 45 or 60 cm. Seeding rate for elite seeds is 60-90 seeds per m^2, for seeds of the first reproduction is 120-180 seeds per m^2, and for seeds of the second reproduction is 180-240 seeds per m^2. Hemp is harvested when the seeds ripen.

This technology is used to grow 30% of hemp in the northern zone, 50% of hemp in the forest and steppe zone and 100% of hemp in the steppe zone. The second technology is used to produce only fiber. Hemp is sown at row width of 7.5 or 15 cm. Seeding rate is 450-500 seeds per m^2. Hemp is harvested after the end of the flowering of the staminate plants. According to which technology of hemp growing is used, different harvesting technologies are employed.

To grow hemp for fiber and seeds direct combining and

swath harvesting are used. For direct combining we use the combine KKY-1.9. The combine cuts plants, threshes and cleans seeds, and binds stems with twine or spreads them out in the field. Hemp is harvested when 75-80% of seeds in inflorescences are ripe as seed shedding losses are minimal. Since not all the seeds are ripe the humidity level of threshed seeds may be as high as 20%.

To avoid damage it is necessary to dry the seeds to decrease the humidity level to 12-13%. The Institute worked out a method of chemical drying of hemp stands by treating them with desiccants during the 7-10 days before the start of harvest. $MgClO_3 \cdot 6\,H_2O$ (10 kg/ha) and Reglon (Diquat) (1 l/ha) are used as desiccants.

Unfortunately, due to the insignificant area devoted to hemp, mass production of hemp combine harvesters is not organized. We consider it possible, through the common efforts of interested firms, to organize joint production of hemp combines. For swath hemp harvesting we use the cutter GK-1.9 which cuts hemp plants, binds them, and throws them down. Binds are threshed by the hemp thresher pK-4.5A. This technology results in greater seed losses and higher-manual labor costs. Hemp grown for fiber only is harvested by the cutter GK-1.9 which cuts plants and spreads them out in the field for dew retting. During dry weather stalks are turned over to obtain even retting.

After dew retting the picking-up machine KB-1 picks up the stalks and binds them. Further operations with loading and unloading binds are connected with high manual labor costs. We also have the technology and machines for rolling retted hemp with parallel arrangement of the stalks.

Hemp-growing and hemp-harvesting technologies in Ukraine differ in many ways from the technologies used in other countries. In Ukraine processing technology is based on treatment of parallelizing hemp stems as in the case of fiber flax. Using this technology we obtain both long and short fiber. About 30% is long fiber and it is used to manufacture the most important products, primarily cordage for marine and river boats.

Conclusions

This process technology is more expensive and requires the expenditure of more labor than technologies in other countries. In the years to come, hemp-growing will be revived in Ukraine and the sphere of hemp usage will change.

Side by side with a traditional use of fiber to manufacture spun products, use of hemp for the pulp, paper, and textile industries will increase considerably.

Forests occupy about 13% of the territory in Ukraine and they are mostly preserved to protect the natural environment. Hemp can play a considerable role in solving the problem of acute shortages of both pulp and paper production. At the Institute we conduct breeding programs aimed at increasing the biological potential of hemp and raising stalk yield to 12-15 t/ha. Hemp harvest and hemp processing technologies will be made considerably simpler and cheaper.

Due to the lack of our own cotton production, and sharp

increases in cotton's price on the world market, the development of the textile and knitting industries of Ukraine will be aimed at utilizing pure hemp and flax fiber, and blends with other natural and synthetic fibers in the manufacture of clothes and other products.

More about hemp: www.hemp.co.uk

Legislation

Although legislation is different around the world it seems that most countries require that, as a potential hemp farmer you have:

- No criminal background
- Have been finger print checked
- Require you state your end use and market contacts
-

Growing Hemp in Australia

New South Wales

New South Wales now issues licenses under a law that came into effect as at 6 November 2008, the Hemp Industry Regulations Act 2008

The NSW Government is calling for license applications to grow industrial hemp and is keen for expressions of interest. Contact Bev Zurbo, Wagga Wagga, (02) 6938 1976, beverley.zurbo@industry.nsw.gov.au. You may visit http://www.dpi.nsw.gov.au/agriculture/field/field-crops/fibres/hemp/commercial-production for further information direct from the Department of Primary Industries where you will find the following documents:

- Industrial hemp - a new crop for NSW (Primefact 801)
- Guidelines for the preparation of licence applications under the Hemp Industry Act 2008 (NSW)
- Hemp Industry Act 2008 (NSW) general conditions of licence
- Application for a licence under the Hemp Industry Act 2008 (NSW)

Queensland

Get a license in **Queensland**:
http://www.dpi.qld.gov.au/26_14354.htm
And learn more about Industrial Hemp In Queensland
(though the contacts are out of date – contact us for more
up to date contacts)
http://www.dpi.qld.gov.au/26_14356.htm

Tasmania

If you are in **Tasmania**, then your best resource is:
http://www.dpiw.tas.gov.au/inter,nsf/WebPages/TTAR-
5R86BK?open

Western Australia

If you are in **Western Australia** then your best resource is:
http://www.agric.wa.gov.au/PC_90019.html

Victoria

If you are in **Victoria**
Department of Primary Industries.
http://new.dpi.vic.gov.au/home

USA

Growing hemp in the USA?

I recommend this reading this report by the Oregon State
University:
http://extension.oregonstate.edu/catalog/html/sb/sb681/

Canada
Growing hemp in Canada?

A great overview on Commercial Hemp Cultivation in Canada "An Economic Justification" by David Marcus may be found here.

The hemp industry seems to be growing most successfully in Alberta in conjunction with the Alberta Research Council. (http://www.arc.ab.ca/)

If you are in Manitoba then the latest crop growing suggestions may be found here:
http://www.gov.mb.ca/agriculture/crops/cropproduction.html

Here are some useful contacts for you:

Industrial Hemp Section Licences and Permits Division, Office of Controlled Substances Drug Strategy and Controlled Substances Programme Healthy Environments and Consumer Safety Branch Health Canada 123 Slater Street, 2nd Floor A. L. 3502A Ottawa, Ontario K1A 1B9 Hemp Office numbers: Phone: (613) 954-6524 Fax: (613) 941-5360 email hemp@hc-sc.gc.ca

Guidance on application to grow hemp in Canada
http://www.hc-sc.gc.ca/hc-ps/pubs/precurs/guid-ligne_direc-eng.php

Application to grow hemp in Canada
http://www.hc-sc.gc.ca/hc-ps/pubs/precurs/hemp_res-chanvr_rech-eng.php

Great fact sheet on hemp in Canada

http://www.agf.gov.bc.ca/speccrop/publications/documents/hemp info.pdf

Italy

Growing hemp in Italy?

Great information is found at
http://www.gruppofibranova.it/eng/hempcrop.htm

Growing Hemp in the UK or 10ha+

We may want to grow hemp as an alternative to your regular crop, just for the returns you get from a contractor. If that is a possibility in your area (UK, France, Germany, Canada, soon Australia) then this following information, prepared by the UK's main and currently only industrial processor Hemp Technology Ltd, will be beneficial.

Industrial hemp now gives the farmer a profitable, alternative spring sown break crop with a guaranteed price and can play a major long term role in cropping plans. The crop can be grown in one of two ways, straw only and straw plus grain.

For a contractor, hemp is worth growing on land of 10 hectare or above and offers benefits that include:

- An Opportunity to earn over £1,000 per hectare with grain and straw production (Dual Cropping).
- Flexible sowing date from mid April to early June.
- Minimal herbicide use (Glyphosate pre drilling). No other chemicals required.
- Price set before sowing giving the grower certainty against a background of wildly fluctuating prices for the alternative crops.
- Hemp's growth rate helps clear the ground of resistant weeds like black grass and bromes.
- Good for rotation complete change from peas, beans, and rape.
- Hemp's deep rooting system is good for soil structure.

- Ideal after late sugar beet and vegetables.
- Spreads the work load direct drill wheat after hemp.
- Minimal slug activity after hemp compared with oil seed rape

Here is text from Hemp Technology, a Company in the UK that contracts for both hemp seed and fibre. Again, much of this information is relevant to you, wherever you are.

If you are in the UK, you may also apply for a license to grow hemp directly from the home office www.homeoffice.gov.uk and for further information see http://www.businesslink.gov.uk/bdotg/action/detail?itemId=1082 224347&type=RESOURCES&lang=en

AGRONOMY

Hemp is an annual crop. Planted in late Spring when soil temperatures are warming up, it achieves a remarkable rate of growth often reaching a height in excess of 3 metres by August. Following harvest the crop is stored by the grower prior to delivery to our factory where the straw is processed and the outer fibres separated from the woody inner core. Until now the processing method required the hemp straw to be retted in the field (retting is the bacterial process that starts to break down the lignin and pectin that holds the fibres together) but the new factory can process un-retted straw. This de-risks hemp growing as the time between cutting and baling can be much shorter and also considerably increases the yield potential as cutting can be delayed and field losses are much reduced. A cutting period of mid to late August will allow baling 2 to3 weeks later, so growers can expect to clear their fields by mid-September.

Previous Cropping

Hemp has an excellent role to play in a number of rotational situations with its twin advantages of late drilling window and good weed control. The two broad categories of use are:

In a cereal rotation as an alternative to the main combinable break crops of rape & pulses.

As a following crop to late cleared root & vegetables, where hemp gives time to prepare the ground rather than being forced to muddle in earlier drilled crops. Our latest sown crop in 2008 was drilled on 12 June and yielded 5.5T/ha.

Seed

The seed, about the size of a peppercorn, should be sown at a rate to achieve a plant population of approximately 150 stems per square metre. This is essential to produce thin stems and good quality fibre. Hemp seed is light & fragile and some air seeders can be very aggressive, damage can be avoided by slowing down fan speeds whilst still achieving good distribution.

Drilling

Hemp should be drilled after the risk of hard frosts has passed and when soil temperatures have reached 10°C plus. This can normally be expected from the third week of April onwards and crops have been drilled successfully up to the beginning of June. Leave a one metre gap round the headland, this will help with inspection of the crop and facilitates harvesting.

A successful hemp crop depends **entirely** on good establishment.

Like all small seeded spring crops it requires a well prepared and friable seedbed. Endeavour to conserve moisture and drill into moisture rather than into a dry seedbed in the hope that it will rain soon.

On all but the lightest soils, land should be ploughed in the Autumn and left to overwinter. Emergence should occur 5-7 days after drilling. Crops that establish quickly and evenly will rapidly grow away from any pest and weed problems. In a dry spring careful attention must be given to moisture retention. Hemp will not penetrate through soils that are compacted or capped so drilling depth (normally 2-3cms) and soil conditions are critical.

Pigeons are a serious pest at the very early stage of plant growth. They must be kept off from drilling day until the plant is past the cotyledon stage and has the first two true leaves. This will occur in the space of 7 to 10 days.

Fertiliser

Nitrogen is a vital component of yield. Depending on soil indices we would recommend up to the following of phosphate and potash :-
HEAVY SOILS 112 N 60 P 120 K KGS/HECTARE
LIGHT SOILS 112 N 60 P 150 K KGS/HECTARE

Hemp is not a greedy crop and returns a substantial quantity of nutrients to the soil. As Hemp thrives on organic matter there may be good opportunities both agronomic and financial to utilise farm yard manure or Sewage Biosolids as a source of nutrients. Because of the need to comply with the protocols and audit trails of our end fibre users and the UK environmental regulations, we recommend no applications should be made without prior approval by Hemp Tecnology.

We recommend checking the lime status and avoiding situations where pH is less than 6.5.

Harvest

There are two possible harvest routes, these are:

1. Hemp for straw - mown with specialised cutter or forager & square baled or disc mown and round baled.
2. Dual hemp – both seed and straw are harvested.

Please discuss with us which is the right route for your farm.

1. A) HEMP FOR STRAW – SHORT CUT AND SQUARE BALED

Two methods of cutting have been tried over the last two years, a multi blade cutting system and foraging. After trials it has been determined that foraging is the preferred cutting method for straw only crops, while the multi blade cutter is ideal for use after the crop has been combined for seed.

If individual growers prefer we will accept crops cut with a disc mower but such crops must be round baled. While cutting costs will be cheaper and the cutting of the crop is in the control of the grower storage and transport costs will be higher.

Baling

Once the crop has dried and is bleached with partial retting it is ready to be rowed up and baled.
Permission for baling must be obtained fromHemp Technology agronomist will give the final go ahead.
Most large square balers should be suitable, take care with pressure settings as too high can cause problems for knotting mechanisms. Discussion with manufacturers can be helpful eg. Hesston balers can be fitted with deflectors which prevent straw getting into knotters.

2. DUAL HEMP FOR SEED AND STRAW

Dual hemp provides considerable opportunity for increased margins, but will delay harvesting until September and greater management input will be required to get the timing of the operations correct.
Hemp seed will come off the combine at 16-18% moisture and needs to be dried to 8% moisture within 6 hours.
Recent results have been excellent and the straw left after combining can then be cut with the new multi cutter and square baled (alternatively it can be mown and round baled.) Growers producing a dual crop must have a contract for both parts, if you would like to pursue this route

please contact us for further details. Due to the extra management required for dual cropping we strongly recommend it be done in minimum blocks of 20 hectares.

The remaining information applies to straw produced from all methods.

Storage

Bales should immediately be removed from the field and stored under cover. Stacking on pallets is recommended on anything other than good quality concrete floors as hemp straw is very absorbent.
Please note that bales of hemp do not shed rainwater.
Intake to the factory is a year round operation on a "just in time basis" and a monthly increment in the price is paid.
Please alert the company if you have specific requirements for movement.
If growers are unable to store their entire crop it is intended to provide a storage facility; this will involve delivery direct from the field with a payment package to reflect the costs involved.

Haulage

Hemp Technology can usually recommend a specialist haulier but growers are welcome to find their own. Payment for straw is on a delivered factory price; some guidance on price is given in the appendix but each situation needs to be costed individually. All incoming loads must be booked in and must be sheeted if at risk of rain.

Straw Quality

The grower is responsible for delivery to the factory where every load is tested to ensure suitability for processing. We would encourage all growers to check their bales before despatch as rejected bales are a waste of expensive haulage and are subject to a disposal charge at the factory.

The main points to watch for are:

a. Moisture Content – we aim for 16 % and can accept up to 18 % with deductions. This has proved very achievable over the years, but watch for wet patches when baling e.g. on headlands and ensure safe storage.

b. Weed Content – a good stand of hemp will allow very little weed competition to survive but in conditions of poor establishment weed can be a problem. Please try to avoid baling any patches of weeds and do not send in weedy bales, as we cannot process them.

c. Stones – These can cause damage in our factory, please tailor field operations to avoid baling up stones. Deductions will be made for stone contamination, in extreme cases there may be rejections.

d. Plastic is, thankfully, not a common problem but one that causes major difficulties for our fibre customers. Please take care to ensure fields and particularly gateways are clear of all plastic and other detritus.

Following Crop

Hemp is an excellent break crop providing a good barrier to pests and diseases. It has been of particular use as a break crop in situations where resistant grass weeds are becoming a problem. Its deep roots are very beneficial for soil structure. The majority of our growers follow hemp with a different crop but some have repeated hemp for several years without any apparent difficulties. Where following Hemp with autumn cereals growers have successfully direct drilled with heavy cultivator drills. Slug activity after hemp is minimal compared with oil seed rape.

Licensing

The term Industrial Hemp is applied to varieties of Cannabis sativa that have been specifically produced by plant breeders to have a THC level (tetra hydro cannabinnol) of 0.2% or less. THC is the psychoactive drug in Cannabis, which in a marijuana plant would be nearer 10 – 15%. However, visually
hemp plants are identical to illicitly grown cannabis plants and can therefore be attractive to drug dealers/users despite the very low THC content. We operate a licencing system as an agent of the Home Office whereby growers apply to Hemp Technology and we consider each application.

Pricing and Viability

Seed price is £3.60 per kilo (£3.80 per kilo for varieties for dual hemp) seed grown for Hemp Technology must be purchased from Hemp Technology. The recommended sowing rate is 37kgs per hectare.

Buy back prices for the straw from harvest 2010 are as follows based on price per tonne of straw delivered factory:

HARVEST £115.00 JANUARY £129.50 MAY   £135.50
OCTOBER £125.00 FEBRUARY £131.00 JUNE £137.00
NOVEMBER £126.50 MARCH £132.50 JULY £138.50
DECEMBER £128.00 APRIL £134.00 AUGUST £140.00

Hemp, in common with all agricultural crops, can show wide variations in yield from season to season.
As part of the Company's supply management they reserve the right, when yields are in excess of 7.5 t/ha, to delay movement of the excess into the period September to December of the following year.

Ex farm prices for hemp grain dried and dressed to contract specifications are as follows;

SEPTEMBER £460.00 JANUARY £472.00 MAY £484.00
OCTOBER £463.00 FEBRUARY £475.00 JUNE £487.00
NOVEMBER £466.00 MARCH £478.00 JULY £490.00
DECEMBER £469.00 APRIL £481.00 AUGUST £493.00

2010 HEMP GROSS MARGIN

The following tables give some indications of gross margins. We have used our best estimates of subsidy levels, yields and prices – please feel free to substitute your own figures. Also consider with Hemp:

Excellent opportunity for controlling grass weeds (especially useful in resistant situations.)
Fewer Field Operations, in particular spraying.
No Combining Requirements – Unless doing dual Hemp in which case higher margins
Prices Based on Contractors – Opportunities to row up & bale in house can considerably increase margins.
Opportunities in Organic Situations.
Hemp may qualify for other environmental schemes, please check with your advisor.
A number of growers have commented on improved yields after hemp than after other break crops.

Gross Margin Per Hectare of Hemp and Alternative Crops

The table below shows the gross margin that can be expected for different yields of hemp compared with alternative break crops. Like all crops the yield can vary depending on the weather and growing conditions. In good years yields of 9 tonnes per hectare have been achieved but an average of 7.5 tonnes per hectare is more likely.

	W Rape	W Beans	S Rape	S Beans	Peas	S Barley	Linseed	Hemp		
Aid	0	37	0	37	37	0	0	0	0	0
Yield	3.5	4.0	2.0	3.5	4.0	6.0	2.0	6.0	7.5	9.0
Crop Value	220	130	220	130	225	110	255	132.5	132.5	132.5
Return	**770**	**557**	**440**	**492**	**937**	**660**	**510**	**795**	**994**	**1193**
Seed	45	60	50	80	125	60	85	137	137	137
Fertiliser	186	60	123	60	90	123	123	155	155	155
Chemicals	195	105	78	88	120	98	72	13	13	13
Cutting	30	30	30	30	30	30	30	60	60	60
Raking	0	0	0	0	0	0	0	10	10	10
Baling	0	0	0	0	0	0	0	66	82	99
Drying/Conditioning	7	8	4	7	8	12	4	0	0	0
Total	463	263	285	265	373	323	314	441	457	474
Gross Margin	**307**	**294**	**155**	**227**	**564**	**337**	**196**	**354**	**537**	**719**

NB. Figures printed on this page are a guide for comparison only and we recommend you insert your own figures especially for fertiliser.

Haulage to Plant Assuming 7.5t/ha

10 mile radius £4/t £30/ha **GM = £507**
30 mile radius £10/t £75/ha **GM = £462**
50 mile radius £12/t £90/ha **GM = £447**
100 mile radius £15 £112/ha **GM = £425**

2010 DUAL HEMP (STRAW & SEED) GROSS MARGINS

Dual hemp is produced for straw and seed both of which are on contract to Hemp Technology. The straw will go to Halesworth for processing by Hemp Technology and the seed will go to Braham & Murray for cold pressing for human consumption under the "Good Oil" Brand name.

Braham & Murray will contract directly with growers for the grain produced from a dual crop.

Dual Hemp Gross Margin per Hectare

The table below shows the gross margin that can be expected from a yield of 6.0 tonnes of straw and 1.2 tonne of grain per ha. Yields of up to 7.0 tonnes of straw and 1.70 tonnes of grain per hectare have been achieved resulting in a gross margin of well over £1000 per hectare.

Tonnes Straw per hectare **6.0**
Tonnes Grain per hectare **1.2**
Straw Revenue March Price £132.50/tonne 795
Grain Revenue March Price £478.00/tonne 574
Total Revenue 1,369
Variable Costs
Seed 137
Fertiliser 155
Chemical 13
Combining 60
Cutting 60

Raking 10
Baling 66
Dressing & Drying 48
Total Costs 549

Gross Margin Before Haulage 820

Haulage to Plant

10 mile radius £4/t £24/ha   **GM = £796**
30 mile radius £10/t £60 **GM = £760**
50 mile radius £12/t £72 **GM = £748**
100 mile radius £15/t £90 **GM = £730**
More than 100 miles £24/t £144 **GM = £676**

The above is based on combining, cutting with the multi-cutter and then square baling.

NB. Figures printed on this page are a guide for comparison only and may not be actual

Uses of hemp in Europe

For up-to-date reports on various hemp markets see www.hemp.co.uk or www.TheHempBuilder.com or www.hempplastic.com (plastic raw material)

You will find reports on:

- **Hemp Plastics**
- **Hemp Textiles**
- **Hemp Bodycare**

and more!

If you prefer a more structured approach and support in creating your own personalized business plan then contact me via www.TheHempConsultant.com

"in contrast to many other crops, especially other renewable resources such as canola or flax, economic loss due to infestation of hemp by pests and diseases is minimal"

Just like with any crop, nutrient and pest problems must be expected when hemp is continuously cultivated in monoculture

Cotton and soy, the two hemp substitute crops, are characterized not only by their enormous demand for pesticides, but also by the toxicity of the respective pesticides in use.

Here are some facts for you to consider in the potential growing market.

How much agricultural land is there left to grow on? 2006>2020

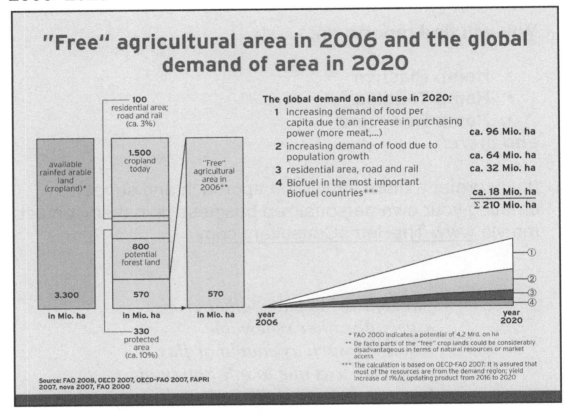

Source: FAO 2008, OECD 2007, OECD-FAO 2007, FAPRI 2007, nova 2007, FAO 2000

Uses of hemp in Europe

For up-to-date reports on various hemp markets see www.hemp.co.uk or www.TheHempBuilder.com or www.hempplastic.com (plastic raw material)

You will find reports on:

- **Hemp Plastics**
- **Hemp Textiles**
- **Hemp Bodycare**
and more!

If you prefer a more structured approach and support in creating your own personalized business plan then contact me via www.TheHempConsultant.com

"in contrast to many other crops, especially other renewable resources such as canola or flax, economic loss due to infestation of hemp by pests and diseases is minimal"

Just like with any crop, nutrient and pest problems must be expected when hemp is continuously cultivated in monoculture

Cotton and soy, the two hemp substitute crops, are characterized not only by their enormous demand for pesticides, but also by the toxicity of the respective pesticides in use.

Here are some facts for you to consider in the potential growing market.

How much agricultural land is there left to grow on? 2006>2020

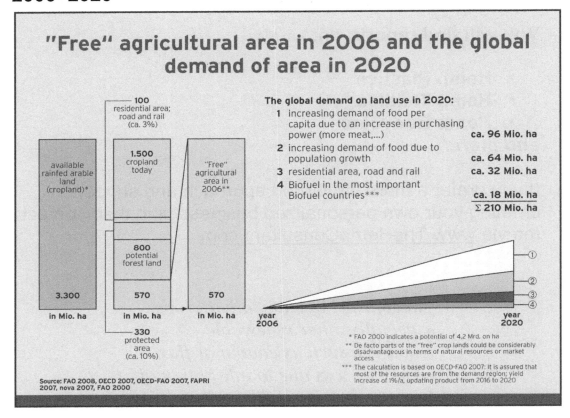

"Free" agricultural area in 2006 and the global demand of area in 2020

The global demand on land use in 2020:

1 increasing demand of food per capita due to an increase in purchasing power (more meat,...)   ca. 96 Mio. ha

2 increasing demand of food due to population growth   ca. 64 Mio. ha

3 residential area, road and rail   ca. 32 Mio. ha

4 Biofuel in the most important Biofuel countries***   ca. 18 Mio. ha

Σ 210 Mio. ha

* FAO 2000 indicates a potential of 4,2 Mrd. on ha
** De facto parts of the "free" crop lands could be considerably disadvantageous in terms of natural resources or market access
*** The calculation is based on OECD-FAO 2007: It is assured that most of the resources are from the demand region; yield increase of 1%/a, updating product from 2016 to 2020

Source: FAO 2008, OECD 2007, OECD-FAO 2007, FAPRI 2007, nova 2007, FAO 2000

Something to consider - Global land use for food production 2006-7

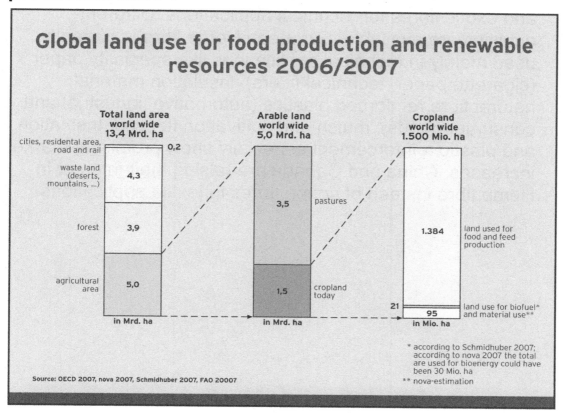

Where is hemp grown today, how much and why?

Today, China, Canada and Europe are the main Hemp cultivation areas in the world. In 2008 the total cultivation area in the European Union was around 15,000 ha – in 2009 we expect this to have increased to18,000 ha. These areas will produce around 24,000 t Hemp fibres and 29,000 t respectively. All by-products like shivs (woody part of the Hemp stem) and dust are used. The main countries for Hemp production are France, UK, Germany, The

Netherlands and Poland. Hemp fibres, ready to use in your biobased products are price competitive to other domestic and exotic fibres for technical applications. Different qualities are available. European Hemp fibre is currently used mainly in technical applications like speciality paper (cigarette paper, technical filters), insulation material, natural fibre reinforced plastics (automotive, industrial and consumer goods), mulch and cultivation fleeces. Insulation and plastic reinforcement especially show promising market increases. China and Canada are raising their interest in Hemp fibre instead of cotton fibres in textile applications.

Hemp and Flax

Flax, also known as linseed, is another bast fibre crop. Hemp and flax crops are used for both their fibres and seeds. Both flax and Hemp fibres are viable alternatives to more conventional fibre crops. The development of the Hemp and flax industry in Europe over the last ten years is directly related to a growing market for plant fibres. There are many figures related to Flax that are available and often bank managers recognize Flax more than they do hemp. Explaining how similar they are may assist.

Price Index of Hemp and Flax 2003-2010

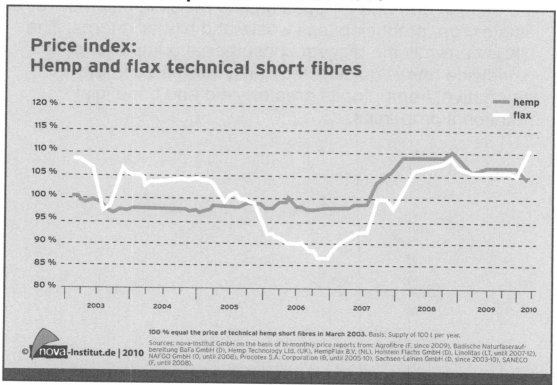

Price index:
Hemp and flax technical short fibres

100 % equal the price of technical hemp short fibres in March 2003. Basis: Supply of 100 t per year.

Sources: nova-Institut GmbH on the basis of bi-monthly price reports from: Agrofibre (F. since 2009), Badische Naturfaserauf-bereitung BaFa GmbH (D), Hemp Technology Ltd. (UK), HempFlax B.V. (NL), Holstein Flachs GmbH (D), Linolitas (LT, until 2007-12), NAFGO GmbH (D, until 2008), Procotex S.A. Corporation (B, until 2005-10), Sachsen-Leinen GmbH (D, since 2003-10), SANECO (F, until 2008).

© nova-Institut.de | 2010

Hemp Seed & Flax Yield comparison

Flax Seed	Hemp Seed
approximately 800 kg/ha yields vary from 500 to 2500kg/ha	approximately 900kg/ha yields of up 2000kg/ha have been recorded.

See bonuses for further characteristics of Hemp and Flax

As these old crops are rediscovered by industry, economical and environmentally sustainable processing technologies are being developed. New machinery has increased the viability of long and short fibre crops. Recent increase in demand for seed makes possible dual use for a single crop, producing less waste and higher returns. The UK is currently the biggest consumer and importer of flax worldwide and is quickly becoming interested in the alternative, hemp, for its greater yield and beneficial nutritional properties.

KNOW YOUR MARKET?
THEN SOURCE
YOUR SEED FROM
www.hemp.co.uk
or
email:
info@hemp.co.uk

TO GROW AND PRE-SELL YOUR CROP – WE TAKE CARE OF THE MARKET!

Interview with Klara Marosszeky.

Klara has experience growing a number of small (1-2 hectare) industrial hemp crops and is currently preparing for a 100ha crop. In this interview you may enjoy Klara's insights and perspective on growing hemp on a small scale.

Hemp for fibre is useful if you want to build your own house. Yes, you can grow your own hemp crop and turn that into a house with the addition of a simple binder. See www.TheHempBuilder.com for more information including the ebook on how to grow your own house from hemp co-written by Klara and this Author.

Klara – Growing

P: Growing hemp starts from the seed. What seed do you need to start?
K: Seed needs to be certified as low THC seed

P:What does that mean?
K: It means that the THC level in the seed cannot be higher than 0.5% in NSW. There are a number of places you can source seed from once you have certification. It can be bought in under license from Europe or Canada (you must have a license to do this).

P:Where do you get those licenses from?

K: From the Department of Primary Industries or equivalent in each state

P:The other option is?
K: To try and source seed in Australia, these are the 2 options for people who just want to get ready to grow. If you are growing for seed, you would only need approx. 3 kg of seed per hectare, and you plant the seed approx 1-1.5 m apart. If you are growing for fibre you are planting between 30-40kg of seed per hectare. So there is a very big difference in the growing patterns. For growing industrial hemp for fibre you will grow the plants incredibly close together so that you are producing a lot of stem rather than a lot of leaf. If you are growing for seed then you want the plants further apart so you have a lot of branching. Some people copice the plants when they get to about knee high. So between the 4th and 7th node of the plant they cut or 'tip' the plant back at that point so that you get more branching and more seed heads. In Australia we have not grown dual crop as yet, but if you are wanting that you would want to grow a crop that is not too tall, so you would be growing a seed crop planting out at 1-1.5m apart and as you would be harvesting the stem out as well, it would be slightly more difficult to manage because of branching. If you are growing hemp just to build an average 3 bed home for yourself then you would need to grow a minimum of 1 hectare of hemp. From that you would get enough fibre to build a moderate dwelling and maybe a small shed. You would be definitely planting at the 30-40kg rate.

P:I have got my seed and am raring to go? What kind of land do I need?

K: Hemp can be grown on a variety of different soils, however it definitely prefers some sorts of soils. So, it would be most happy in a fertile well manured paddock whether you have done that by growing a green manure crop before you planting hemp seed, you could do that by planting pidgeon peas or lucerne and prepare the soil in that kind of way. Or you will need to add fertiliser to adjust the soil to PH 6. It is possible to grow in clay soils, however you will have to mound it up, so you will have to grow it in mounded rows. Other than that what hemp requires is a nice loose bed to be planted into to allow the tap root to move through the soil easily.

P: Does it need access to much water?
K: Yes it does need access to regular water, it does not need a lot. But if you don't have either good subsoil moisture if you are dry land farming it , and then some rain every 3-4 weeks you will only get a moderate crop. You will still get a good yield if you have good sub soil moisture. Generally speaking if you are planting and you do have irrigation, you would make sure that the seed is kept moist during the germination process, then it should be irrigated fortnightly, you shouldn't let the plants get stressed, so you need to irrigate if you have a prolonged dry spell or the THC level will start to creep up.

P: I believe you need water at the very beginning as well when it is just sprouting?
K: Absolutely that is the water for the germination process, once the seed has been damp then you need to keep the seed moist so it can keep that full germination process. If it gets wet and then dries off you will get seed death. If you

plant it into soil that doesn't have any sub-soil moisture then you have to irrigate regularly for the first 6 weeks.

P: How much land do I need if I want t o consider growing hemp? For seed, for fibre, for my own home?Where is the economical level to growing hemp?
K: It does depend on why you are wanting to grow hemp. If you are growing hemp because you are wanting to live in a sustainable kind of way, then if you grew 1 hectare of dual purpose crop, you could harvest the seed, and providing it were legal to eat the seed then you would have a seed source from which you could make a grain and you would expect to get 1 tonne of seed off your hectare, and about 10 tonnes yield of dry fibre, which would give you ample for building a home, we are looking at about 3 tonnes in a small size home.

P:I have my land and my seed, how do I first prepare the land
K: Some months, ideally before you were planning to plant, you would have turned in the paddock and you would be working it to get rid of weeds, and making any adjustments to the soil that you thought needed to happen, so you would be manuring, if you started this process a couple of months before planting you would get a really good reduction of weeds in that area of soil, which would enable the hemp to get a really good head start on any weeds coming through. So, you are preparing it to make a fine seed bed and planting directly into that at a depth of about 1cm or slightly more.

P: What machines would I need for this process and where would I get them from?

K: Well the tiniest would be a rotary hoe that you might be able to hire from a landscaping company or something like that and if you were growing 1 hectare and were willing to do that over a couple of weekends that would be a very manageable thing to do. That would be the lowest cost way to do it if you don't have access to any farming equipment such as tractor, plough, disks to prepare the land in that kind of way then a rotary would be the way to go.

P: The next level up would be if my neighbour had a tractor, and I could borrow it, what would I need to put on the tractor?
K: I have only ever done it with disk ploughs on a 2 hectare site broad acre planted because I did not have access to a seeder. However you can get access to small seeders which are very economical I think you can buy one for less than $3-400 if you are doing it on a small scale so that you can get quite a precise planting. It can be grown by broad acre, throwing the seed out and learning to do that in a really even way, which is how I planted my first 2 hectares.

P: Is there a particular brand of these seeders or rotary hoes that make a difference?
K: I find the older the better, I have always worked with ancient machines on farms, in a ways simple machines, unless you have a simple harvester that is designed for hemp, the older and simpler the machine, with fewer turning parts the better it is for using it. Throughout the world a whole lot of simple technologies are used for growing hemp.

P: I have grown my seed 1.5cm deep and 1.5m apart and now what am I waiting for? Do I need any chemicals, fertiliser, pesticides? Do I need them?

K: You don't need any herbicides, providing your field is well prepared you don't need any of these things, you might struggle with weeds if it is not well prepared and if it has been left to lie fallow for a couple of months. Pesticides, there are known pests to hemp in Australia, we don't have any problems with pests, no pesiticides are necessary, as it has not been an issue with growing hemp in Australia, it may be different when we get big mono cultures. It would be recommended that you fertilise in some kind of way, and that can be a very low tech way. In the first site we grew on I did add some lime to adjust the ph, as it was incredibly poor soil, we turned in rotting lucerne bails to the soil and added dynamic lifter and grew it in that way about as low tech as you can get.

P: What are the latest requirements for land?

K: The legislation in NSW specifies that the owner of the land can't have had any criminal conviction, secondly that the site is going to be monitored, that there is a house near by and it is going to be looked after, that the crop is not visible from the road although that would be something worth challenging if your circumstances required it. The first crop I ever grew was fully visible and I approached DPI and said because it was very visible would it be ok if instead I publicised where the site was and worked with police so that people would see that it was a hemp demonstration crop, so there are all sorts of ways of going around the legislation or working within the legislation. People are often concerned that you would have to have incredibly high fencing, however that is not a reality generally a 3 barbed wire fence is ample with a gate into it, you do have to display that it is a licensed area and limited access. Anyone who will be working on your hemp crop, you would need to list as a close associates on your license and then those people have to give permission for a police check as well.

P: How do I know if my crop is ready for harvesting?
K: Depending on the purpose of the crop, the end use, you would harvest at different times

P: So lets start with seed
K: I am not an authority on this but my understanding is you are going to lose half of your seed to the birds, or half of your seed being green so you are really choosing when will be the optimal time to get out the majority of seed and I haven't personally harvested a crop for seed, but working with the Tea Tree farmers I believe we have the equipment to take off the tips of the plants.

P: And fibre:
K: Your seed may be governed by a non-propogation agreement, so if it is Australian seed it will generally have this, which means it needs to be harvested prior to seeds heading. Ideally you would harvestrf prior to seeds heading for fibre anyway. In the fibre process it is a pain in the neck to have seed in the picture. If you are growing for textiles, you would be harvesting out as soon as the male plants start to die. If you are growing for building materials it is all good! Whenever the weather allows you to get the drying time.

P: What machines do I need to harvest a small 1ha crop?

K: If I was havesting 1 hectare for myself, I would recommend a 4 stroke brushcutter just because they are more energy efficient and they have a blade and are powerful. It is quite a simple process to harvest, I have harvested up to 2 hectares by hand. It takes about a day, one person picking up the hemp with a ute, and one person harvesting swapping roles as required. You just walk along and sweep along with the brushcutter and it falls over very neatly and the other person picks it up and puts it on the ute. Very manageable.

P: What can go wrong in any of those processes?
K: If you are seeding, you could put the seed too deeply in the soil and you won't get germination or if you don't have irrigation and the seed is not kept moist in the first part, you won't get a successful crop. In the growing, really it is lack of irrigation that is your biggest problem there provided you have prepared your soil. The riskiest part of growing hemp is harvesting process. It is actually relatively easy to grow hemp if your soil is well prepared because it is a really strong plant, many people talk of it as a weed. It is risky because if you are wanting to get the hemp for building purposes you are wanting to get it out of the field without leaf on it. The legislation also prefers that, and you are also wanting to get it out dry. Once you have started touching the hemp and you have cut it off you are exposing the hemp to moisture, and hemp has a phenomenal capacity to absorb moisture from the field, so my initial preference unless you are living somewhere with very long drying days where you could just harvest it as whole stem, leave it, rake it a couple of times to take off the leaf, and then you can bail it or take it out as whole stem.

P: How long would you have to leave it for?

K: If you are living somewhere and harvest it at a time of year when you have long drying days like in Ashford, NSW it takes 2-3 days. If you have dew happening (May or June) it will take up to 10 days of drying time providing you don't get any rain, even then you may have difficulty with the head – the dense leaf at the top of it.

P: What happens if it does rain in the middle of all that and you weren't expecting it?

K: It's going to be sitting in the field a lot longer and you will then have the danger the longer that Is out there that you will have a lot of retting happening, and then you will get fibre separation. For building material, and because I am using the whole stem, and because it is possible to use the whole stem you actually want to get it out of the field intact. In the past I have worked with harvesting it green and getting it out of the field green using a forage harvester and taking it out to dry it. I took an experiment and dried it in the gas dryers that the tea tree industry uses. As the moisture in the stem is very low while it is a standing crop, when you are piling it all up on top of each other that is when the moisture level can really grow. That is why on a commercial level I prefer to green harvest to take that risk out of it of potentially months of being in the fields.

P: So, if it looks like it is going to rain then go and find a gas dryer?

K: Yes, or make a solar drier, just put it under a tin roof and you keep turning it it will dry without any problem and with 2 hectares of quantity that is manageable.

P: What else that can go wrong?

K: Birds are a problem with seeds. With storing seed, rats can be a problem. You have to store hemp away from moisture, because it absorbs moisture. Most animals won't touch it.

P: Anything else about growing hemp on a small scale
K: I would certainly encourage people to look at biodynamics on a small scale as it is such a cheap way to improve the soil.

P: Where would they find out about that?
K: By contacting anyone in that field Victorian Biodynamic Farming Association apply BD500, very inexpensive way of improving the soil.

P: Have you done that yourself:
K: I was growing on very poor soils and I have a friend that was growing biodynamically so I was monitoring what was going on in his farm and spoke to him because the soil I was growing on was really depleted it was just a sandy loam it had nothing left in it.

P: You have said why you don't want to ret for the building industry, but what are the reasons you would want to ret the stalk on the field?
K: You would do that if you wanted to make textiles, fibreglass replacement, plastics, paper or for a multitude of uses. There is lots of uses for the outside fibre.

P: How would ret in field?
K: There are supposedly machines that do that, but I believe they are not efficient yet. The other way is to field ret. It is left in the field with the dew on it (or irrigated), and

it is then a rotting process. The moulds cause a separation of the outside fibre from the inside fibre. If you are doing that on a cottage scale, then after 3-6 weeks you would gather up the stems give them a shake and the inside herd would fall out which would leave you with the outside fibre. That is how it was done in China where it was done on a large scale. It depends on the quality of fibre your market requires. In Europe they use steam explosion methods and other techniques but they are very expensive. There are new enzyme methods also in R&D phase. If on your 2 hectare block you were really wanting to maximize every opportunity from growing your hemp crop you would probably ret some of it and use it to make ropes, paper etc. In the building material you can either use the inside part of it or the whole stem.

P: When you leave it in the field to ret and separate, you can use both parts of it?
K: Yes, and the same process happens if you put it in a pond.

P: Was that done because it was very dry?
K: Yes it needs some moisture. It was also done like that in some areas because it was a more manageable process and it minimised losses because you might have quite a high percentage of loss in field retting. The thing that has limited pond retting expanding is the technologies and concerns of nutrification of the water and letting that water back out into the environment, one way of getting around that would be to dilute and use that water on your land with crops etc. My understanding is that pond retting is very effective

P: Pond retting is basically that you take the fibre off the floor in to a pond or big tank of water and leave it for how long?

K: Not sure, depends on the weather, I left some in my fish pond in the summer and within a week it was off , when cooler it takes longer.

P: If you were really wanting to low tech separate hemp, you could do what the Japanese do which is they immerse it for 1 day and then keep under damp cloths for 2 days and then they peel them back and it separates relatively easily. The longer it is left to ret, the harder it is to separate, or the tighter it is - just like bark on a tree. Another thing about pond retting is that it doesn't matter how long it has been since it was cut it will still ret.

P: Further onsite harvesting for building: you have told me you need to have the stem in smaller sections. How do we do that?

K: I have done that with a fibre mulcher, and that chops it very effectively. It can be rented or hired easily. You push stems through the top of it and it comes out the end, it's easy!

P: Thank-you so much for your time. I trust this will be of use to the readers. Where can they find out more about growing hemp for building a home?

K: www.TheHempBuilder.com

Video Links

Watch how the French build with hemp
http://www.youtube.com/watch?v=CpQQ448IoIg

See the Hemp Lotus Eco Elise car in action here
http://www.youtube.com/watch?v=cOCm8CNsvWg

Watch a video from South African Hempster Tony
http://www.youtube.com/watch?v=NF87CSzskMA

Hempsters plant a seed with Woody Harrelson
http://www.youtube.com/watch?v=f9hN6Ql1UEw

Hemp Shopping

All from **www.hemp.co.uk**

Hemp Foods

Hemp Protein Powder

This Hemp Protein Powder has a gourmet nutty flavor that tastes so good you can eat it straight from the jar. Use it to create delicious shakes, add it to juices, smoothies and green drinks. Buy 100% raw, cold milled Hemp Protein Powder from www.hemp.co.uk

Hemp Seed Nut

Otherwise known as shelled hemp seeds – these are the tastiest and most pure way to enjoy the drug-free nutritional qualities of hemp seeds. A complete protein (35%), omega 6 and omega 3 Essential Fatty Acids (35%) and is a source of GLA (1%). These are delicious sprinkled on salads, cereals, yogurt or cooked grains. I eat it straight from the bag! This hemp seed nut is cold mechanically pressed and packaged without additives or preservatives and grown without herbicides or pesticides from Non-GMO hemp seed. So what are you waiting for? Buy now from here!

Hemp Seed Nut Butter

Like peanut butter or tahini, but tastes better and is much better for you as nature's source of complete protein (35%) and Omega 6 & 3 Essential Fatty Acids (35%). May be sprad on breads, bagels, crackers and croissants.. So get some now!

Hemp Seed Oil

Certified Organic Hemp Seed Oil is nature's richest source of the Essential Fatty Acids (75%) and is a rich source of GLA (3%). Hemp Seed Oil is preferable over flax seed oil as it offers a good balance of Omega 6 to Omega 3 fatty acids (3.75:1) so it is suitable for life long consumption. And you will have a long life. Tastes a lot better than fish oils with a mild nutty flavour. Can be eaten straight (I do) or added to juices, smoothies, soups and sauces. It is a great base to any salad dressings. Hemp Oil is not ideal for frying. Also available in capsule format. Go to www.hemp.co.uk to buy now.

Hemp Cosmetics

Hemp oil is used as the base of cosmetic products because it helps make the skin feel young, and smooth. Hemp Oil has been shown to improve eczema and other dry skin ailments. Hemp Oil in cosmetics is absorbed by the skin and after a short while of using such products I am sure you will notice the difference yourself. A great range of hemp cosmetics is available via www.hemp.co.uk - shipping worldwide.

Hemp Jewelry

Want to share something special and let them know you care about the planet as much as you do them? You will want to tell that to yourself when you find Phat Hemp's excellent range of Hemp Necklaces, Bracelets, Jewelry for men and women. Lots of one of a kind eco friendly jewelry found at www.hemp.co.uk

Cannabis Seeds

For growing medical marijuana – where legal only. One of the largest Dutch marijuana seed suppliers based in Amsterdam offers of 30 classic strains from the place where high quality breeding has always been an art. Don't waste your time with inferior seeds, buy from www.hemp.co.uk

Got a problem with smoking?

The cannabis coach is here to help you stop smoking cannabis. A 100% guaranteed risk-free program is available at www.hemp.co.uk – please share with anyone that has a problem smoking cannabis.

Hemp Clothing

At the time of going to press we were updating our recommendations for hemp textiles and clothing. You may visit the relevant page at www.hemp.co.uk for more information or email info@hemp.co.uk directly to find what you are looking for.

Hemp Plastics

From the original www.hempplastic.com site you will find opportunities for access to hemp plastic materials, products and more. Go there now!

Hemp Fibre, Industrial Hemp Growing Seeds, Hemp Stalk, Hemp Mulch, Hemp Insulation, Hemp Building Products and more

All available from www.hemp.co.uk

The Hemp Network Business Opportunity

The Time For Hemp Is Now... Join The Hemp Revolution!

The Hemp Network represents the first marketing distribution channel in history that will provide consumers with hemp products on a direct sales and a network marketing platform.

We are in an industry that <u>has been around for thousands of years</u>, with new uses for hemp being constantly developed. The use of hemp is growing dramatically and will continue as more recognized uses occur.

Over the past few years it has become apparent that with the increasing pace of new products hitting the market, there is a need to move those products throughout the world at a very fast rate.

The Hemp Network has been formed to provide a marketing vehicle for massive global distribution of these new products and services as they hit the market, which is imperative to capture market share.

Expectations are that our marketing team will become a major force in the exploding hemp product marketplace... and we are offering individuals like you the opportunity to capitalize on this exploding market.

The Hemp Network offers the winning combination of product, people, management and vision to all work together to create a very large global marketing company with our agents earning income from people spread around the world.

There has <u>never been a more perfect time</u> to take advantage of an industry that has been around for thousands of years, with products derived from hemp being used by millions of people today. Over the past few years it has become apparent that with the increasing pace of new hemp products hitting the market, there is a need to move those products throughout the world at a very fast rate.

Join our very special team and get unique support for your new business!

visit <u>www.hemp.co.uk</u> to be part of the revolution!

Thanks for reading
Growing Hemp For Profit

See you at
www.hemp.co.uk

Other websites:

www.hempplastic.com
www.thehempbuilder.com
www.hempmusic.com

Made in the USA
Middletown, DE
11 November 2018